WHAT EVERY CEO
MUST KNOW ABOUT
RISK

THE DRAGONFLY APPROACH

JUDY LEE & LIENGSENG WEE
COFOUNDERS, DRAGONFLY LLC

WHAT EVERY CEO
MUST KNOW ABOUT
RISK

THE DRAGONFLY APPROACH

First Edition published 2017 by Insight Books, Inc.
New York, NY

ISBN 978-0-692-91380-2

CONTENTS

INTRODUCTION

INTRODUCTION: WHY WE WROTE THIS BOOK

In our 25+ years as practitioners and advisors in risk management, we've seen many changes – the size of shocks, the frequency of surprises, the pervasiveness and degree of awareness of the need for risk management, just to name a few. But some things have not changed, such as the questions CEOs keep asking us about risk management:

- What do I need to know about risk management?
- What's my role in risk management?
- How can we make risk management effective in practice?

In the course of our years of work with CEOs, business line heads and boards of directors, we have distilled some definitive answers to such questions.

We founded Dragonfly to help CEOs, investors and institutions create and manage value under *uncertainty*. We develop sophisticated firm-wide risk management capabilities for any industry or sector, including non-profits and government agencies. We apply *quantitative* risk management methodologies to help clients make smarter strategy decisions and do better investment evaluation and structuring. We help CEOs allocate resources among different risky ventures. We have tested and proven that our frameworks and methodologies work.

We decided to write this book because we felt it would be useful to provide CEOs with a quick, go-to reference for their fundamental questions on risk management. It is substantive and deep enough, but not overly-technical or detailed to the point of being a manual for a risk management specialist. The book answers all the key questions a CEO may have on risk management, such as:

1. What do I need to know about risk management?
   - What is risk?
   - How can I know all the risks my organization faces?
   - Are all risks quantifiable?

2. What's my role in risk management?
   - Should I aim to minimize risk?
   - Should I aim to minimize losses?
   - What's my organization's capacity to take risk?
   - How do I decide my risk appetite?
   - How can risk help me compete better and serve my customers better?

3. How can we make risk management effective in practice?
   - How do I strengthen risk management without stifling the business lines?
   - How do I ensure independence of the risk team and still get buy-in from the organization?
   - How do I design a risk dashboard that's useful in practice?
   - How much of risk management is science and how much is art?

Over the years, we have developed a unique methodology — **The Dragonfly Approach** — that enables CEOs in any industry to understand and manage *all* risks using a *quantitative* framework. We will be sharing key concepts and insights of The Dragonfly Approach in the following chapters.

Instead of answering each of the above questions individually, however, we have structured the book into 9 chapters that cover "What Every CEO Must Know About Risk". This is because while individual CEOs may have differing emphases on the risk issues to which they need answers, *all* CEOs need to know these 9 sets of principles and insights:

1. What Is Risk?
2. Know Your Bets. You Are Always Taking Bets
3. Why All Risks Should Be Quantified
4. All Risks Can Be Quantified
5. How to Quantify and Evaluate Strategic Risk
6. Deciding Your Risk Appetite
7. What's Your Risk Management Philosophy?
8. Why Many Common Risk Management Practices Are Flawed
9. Making Risk Management Effective in Practice

We have developed, tested and refined these 9 principles over our 25+ years of continuous practice in risk management, starting at Bankers Trust in the late 1980s and continuing at Dragonfly which we founded in 2000. Together, the 9 principles constitute The Dragonfly Approach to building effective risk management capabilities for clients in any industry or sector.

Our goal for risk management has always transcended compliance and corporate governance. We believe that risk management should involve a philosophy as well as a set of capabilities to help firms compete better under conditions of uncertainty.

This book synthesizes the risk insights we believe every CEO will find useful. We hope that after you read it, you will begin a valuable dialogue with us about what works and doesn't work for you, as well as whether there are questions you might have that are not addressed in this book. This continual engagement is necessary in a world where change and volatility are the only certainties.

> " We apply *quantitative* risk management methodologies to help clients make smarter strategy decisions and do better investment evaluation and structuring. "

CHAPTER 1

1

WHAT IS RISK?

If we ask ten CEOs to define risk, we will get at least five different answers. While these definitions might be valid for specific purposes, they are inadequate for effective risk management at the CEO or enterprise-wide level.

Under The Dragonfly Approach, **risk is defined as the chance of not meeting your goals**, or more specifically, **as the potential deviation of outcomes compared to your goal** (or target level of outcome).

Risk is best shown as the probability distribution of potential outcomes – see Exhibit 1.1 below:

Exhibit 1.1: The Dragonfly Risk Definition

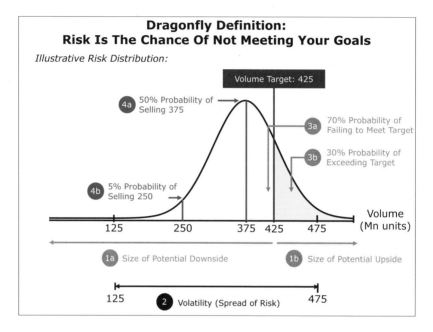

Risk can be described further as:

1. The range of possible outcomes:
    –   The size of potential downside versus the target level, which, in this example, is selling 425 million units (see 1a in Exhibit 1.1); and
    –   The size of potential upside from the target level (see 1b in Exhibit 1.1).

2. The volatility of potential outcomes around the target level (see 2 in Exhibit 1.1). (For risk that looks like a normal distribution, the volatility is the standard deviation of the distribution. This will be discussed in more detail later in this chapter).

3. The cumulative probability of failing to make the target level of the goal (see 3a in Exhibit 1.1), and the converse: the probability of exceeding the target goal level (see 3b in Exhibit 1.1).

4. The different levels of the goal that could be attained and the probability of reaching each level. (See 4a in Exhibit 1.1: we might sell only 375 million units, where the probability of that happening is 50%; and also see 4b: we might sell only 250 million units, where the probability of that happening is 5%).

The complete set of potential outcomes and the associated probabilities is called a risk distribution.

Specify Your Goals

Dragonfly's definition of risk emphasizes the importance of specifying one's goals. In practice, we have come across situations where the CEO, top executives and stakeholders have differing and sometimes un-verbalized goals in mind when assessing risk. This creates confusion and often irreconcilable views.

66 Articulate what your goals are. For each goal, there is a specific risk distribution. 99

Dragonfly recommends using the following framework for specifying your goals and defining risk in your organization (Exhibit 1.2):

Exhibit 1.2: The Dragonfly Framework for Defining Risk

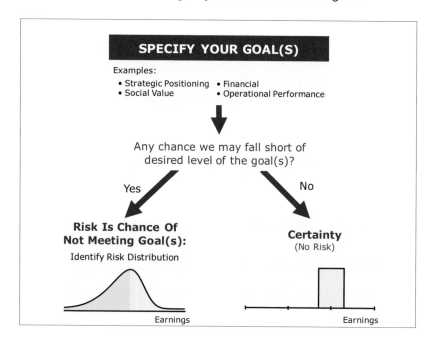

- What goal or goals are we looking at?
- Is the goal risky, i.e. is there a chance that we may fall short of the desired level of the goal?
- If the goal is uncertain, define risk as the chance of not meeting the specific goal. Describe the risk as laid out in the earlier section of this chapter. Ideally, articulate what the risk distribution looks like. For each goal, there is a specific risk distribution.

Risk, Risk Metric, Risk Drivers

A common reason for the confusion over what constitutes risk is that many executives are unclear about the difference between 3 related concepts – **risk**, **risk metrics** and **risk drivers**. Let's clarify each concept:

- **Risk** – as defined earlier, it is the chance of not meeting a specified goal.

- **Risk Metric** – a measure of risk. A common risk metric, particularly useful for financial institutions, is VaR (Value at Risk). It is the magnitude of the shortfall in value (valuation) at the 99th percentile lowest level of the distribution of possible values of a portfolio of assets. Firms may also pick a different level at which to measure VaR, such as 95th percentile or 99.9th percentile.

  There are other risk metrics, of course. (These are discussed further in Chapter 4 on risk quantification). However, it is important to know that VaR is not necessarily the appropriate risk metric for many firms, especially non-financial institutions.

  For now, we want to point out that the appropriate risk metric should generally be the same unit as what is used to measure the goal itself. Hence, if sales is the goal, then the risk metric should be "Sales at Risk".

- **Risk Driver** (or Risk Type) – there are usually several different drivers or causes of risk for any goal. Similarly, one risk driver can cause volatility in more than one goal.

Let's use a hypothetical budget airline to illustrate the importance of distinguishing between risk, risk metrics and risk drivers. Assume our airline has an earnings goal of $300 million. The appropriate definition of risk would be the chance that earnings deviate from the CEO's target. The risk metric should therefore be the level of earnings.

The risk to the earnings could be caused by:

1. A competitor successfully gaining market share at the airline's expense;
2. Price of jet fuel rising above what was used in the CEO's budget; and/or
3. Increase in delays due to aircraft maintenance problems.

In this example, the risk drivers are:

1. Strategic – pricing strategy "bet" that competitors will not undercut prices to grab market share;
2. Financial Market – jet fuel price surging in the commodities market;
3. Operational – failure in operations, such as maintenance required to get aircraft ready for on-time takeoffs.

See Exhibit 1.3 below:

Exhibit 1.3: Risk Distribution of a Budget Airline

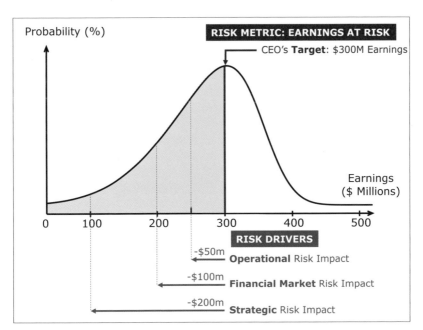

Although these are 3 different causes of risk (i.e. risk drivers), there is only one goal and hence, one defined risk: the chance that we may not meet the $300 million earnings target. So the 3 different risk drivers share the same risk metric – "earnings at risk".

As shown in Exhibit 1.3 above, strategic risk has a downside impact of $200 million; financial market risk has an impact of $100 million; and operational risk, $50 million.

To recap, we use Exhibit 1.3 to distinguish 3 aspects of risk:

  a. Risk Definition – in this case, the risk is defined as the chance of not making the $300 million earnings goal.
  b. Risk Metric – in this case, it is Earnings at Risk (in $ millions).
  c. Risk Drivers – we showed three: strategic, financial market, operational.

We have met many CEOs who were advised to focus on only one risk metric, such as VaR. This is erroneous advice, because VaR works well as a risk metric only when the goal is a valuation target. With our budget airline example, valuation is not the specified goal; earnings is the goal. Hence VaR would not be appropriate.

In other cases, the goal may be sales volume, unit costs, etc. Therefore, it is critical to pick the risk metric that is appropriate for the specified goal. Otherwise, certain risks may be omitted or badly measured. It could also create the misconception that some risks cannot be quantified.

For example, if we had used VaR as the risk metric in an organization where sales volume is the goal in focus, we would not be able to directly quantify the rise of a volume shortfall. Or we might create the false impression that a non-financial goal – sales volume – cannot be quantified.

The Dragonfly Approach requires that we examine every goal individually to determine what the relevant risk metric is.

Recap: What is Risk?

Based on the wide variety of clients and sectors we have worked with, we believe it is imperative that CEOs adopt The Dragonfly Approach's definition of risk — the chance of not meeting your goals. There may be other useful definitions, but none is as practical for the CEO's role in risk management at the enterprise-wide level.

The Dragonfly Approach's definition of risk sets the foundation for robust quantification, using a full distribution of possible outcomes, and linking risk metrics directly to your goals. Defining risk correctly enables you to make smart decisions as well as to manage risk more effectively — topics which we will cover in the coming chapters.

66 The Dragonfly Approach's definition of risk sets the foundation for robust quantification, using a full distribution of possible outcomes, and linking risk metrics directly to your goals. 99

Risk Insights from Chapter 1

What Is Risk?

1. For CEOs: When managing the risks of the enterprise, it is imperative to adopt Dragonfly's definition of risk – the chance of not meeting your goal(s).

2. A risk distribution shows the probability of each level of possible outcome of your goal.

3. It is important to specify each of your goals clearly.

4. Once your goals are specified, select the appropriate risk metrics to use.

5. Finally, identify the risk drivers and quantify the impact of the drivers on the goal(s).

6. It is critical to understand the difference between risk as defined, risk metrics and risk drivers.

CHAPTER 2

KNOW YOUR BETS.
YOU ARE ALWAYS TAKING BETS

So far, we have not come across a CEO – in any sector – fortunate enough to have goals that are guaranteed to be attainable. We believe that **all goals involve uncertainty, which means that as a CEO you are always taking bets. Therefore, as CEO, you need to know what the bets are**.

We first used this expression, *"Know your bets. You are always taking bets"* ten years ago in a presentation to the board of directors of a large, prestigious 100 year-old insurance company. Half the room was aghast and several directors started to protest that we had failed to appreciate that they were a hundred year-old, well-run and conservative institution. It took a couple more minutes before the insight soaked in and a few other directors realized that even as a competent provider of risk protection, an insurance company was taking bets – on mortality, on operating efficiency, and on investment returns, among other things.

We could have said, "All goals are risky, because you are making assumptions about the underlying drivers of success." However, as this episode showed, semantics *do* matter. "Know your bets. You are always taking bets" jolts us into awareness that in managing organizations, we take risks in all the goals we set.

Exhibit 2.1 You Are Always Taking Bets

Whatever Your Goals Are

Goals & Target Set

Success Depends On:

Things that must go right	Things that must not go wrong

Therefore, Goals are Risky

But These Are Uncertain

You Are Always Taking Bets

This awareness is the foundation of effective risk management. This is true not just for businesses, but also for government agencies and non-profits. All organizations take bets in pursuit of their goals.

Strategic Bets

Let's assume we can get everyone to accept that the firm is taking bets. How do we figure out what these bets are?

We have created a useful framework – **The Dragonfly Strategic Bets Framework** – to show that underlying each goal are four key strategic bets: Demand, Capabilities, Competition and Macro / Environment. (See Exhibit 2.2).

Exhibit 2.2: The Dragonfly Strategic Bets Framework

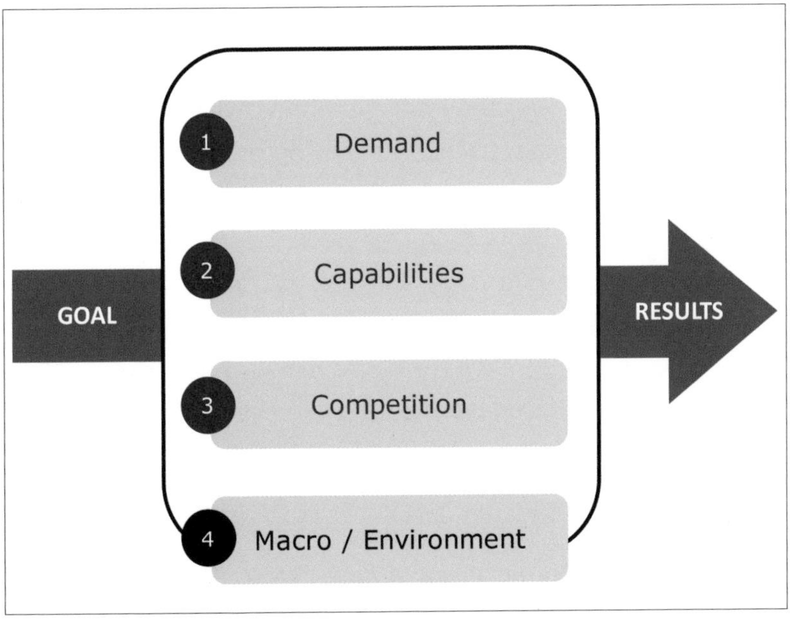

1. Demand Bet
   Any goal is a bet on one or more demand-side factors such as market size, market growth potential, pricing, product attributes, etc.

2. Capabilities Bet

   All goals will include bets on your ability to source, produce and distribute your products/solutions, your cost structure, as well as your ability to continue to provide attractive products to your target market.

3. Competition Bet

   Directly or indirectly, your customers have choices. Worse, sometimes alternatives appear from totally new sources. Hence, your goal is also a bet that you will be able to attain an adequate share of the market that both existing and emerging players are competing with you for.

4. Macro / Environment Bet

   To different degrees, all goals involve taking bets on macro forces such as GDP, GDP growth, regulations, political environment and financial market conditions.

The above framework covers the overarching strategic and macro bets underlying any goal. It is a powerful and quick tool for a first pass at identifying risks. What we have been calling "bets" can also be called risk drivers, risk types or sources of risk.

The Dragonfly Universe of Risk Drivers & Linkages

For a comprehensive and more detailed understanding of *all* the bets an organization takes, we have developed a second framework – **The Dragonfly Universe of Risk Drivers & Linkages.** (See Exhibit 2.3).

Exhibit 2.3: The Dragonfly Universe of Risk Drivers & Linkages

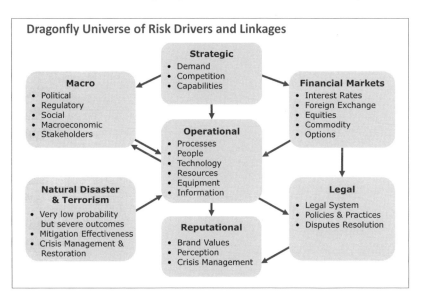

All organizations are exposed to these seven categories of risk drivers, to varying degrees. There may also be some overlap between categories. Also, risk drivers can affect or be affected by other drivers. The seven categories of risk drivers are:

1. Strategic Risk Drivers

   The organization's strategy is a useful overarching context to start identifying all the risk factors underlying its goals. Any strategy involves the following bets:
   - Demand-side bets
   - The nature of the competition
   - The organization's capabilities

   Strategy may also involve:
   - Financial market drivers (covered separately in category 3 below)
   - Macro factors (covered separately in category 4 below)

2. <u>Operational Risk Drivers</u>

   We define operations as how an organization's strategy is implemented, involving processes, people, resources, information, etc. Operational risk is the shortfall or variability in any aspect of operations, compared to targets or requirements.

3. <u>Financial Market Risk Drivers</u>

   Variability in financial market parameters such as interest rates, commodity prices, foreign exchange rates and equity prices are classified collectively as financial market risk drivers.

   Other key financial market risk drivers are credit quality, availability of financing/refinancing and liquidity conditions. An oft-omitted area is the correlation in price movements or relative values among different financial assets. This is also called basis risk.

   Most of us are well aware that financial institutions take huge exposures in this category of risk drivers, as it is their core business. However, non-financial firms, governments and to a substantial degree even non-profits, are also affected by financial market drivers. This is true even though financial market transactions are not their core business.

   All corporate and business strategies require some capital structure and often financial market bets. That is why we may include this risk driver category in category 1 (Strategic Risk Drivers) above, instead of treating it as a separate category (as in #3 here).

4. Macro / Environment Risk Drivers
   Organizations operate within a larger context, and depending on the strategies they pursue, are affected by macro factors such as:
   • Macroeconomic conditions
   • Political conditions
   • Regulatory systems
   • Social norms and preferences
   • Stakeholder concerns

5. Natural Disasters / Terrorism
   This category includes sources of risk that have large and often severe-to-catastrophic impact, but occur with very low probability, e.g., various types of natural disasters, acts of terrorism or sabotage.

6. Legal Risk Drivers
   Organizations operate in different legal systems, affecting how they manage their rights and liabilities. Sources of legal risks include: legal frameworks chosen, agreements made, rights or protections depended upon, actions taken or not taken in legal disputes and the results of these actions.

7. Reputational Risk Drivers
   An organization has a certain desired institutional image as well as desired brand attributes. Typical sources of reputational risks include events, incidents, actions taken or not taken, how the organization manages in a crisis, how it handles disputes with any of its stakeholders, etc.

Customizing The Dragonfly Universe of Risk Drivers & Linkages

In our twenty-five years of work in risk management, we have used and tested this general framework for identifying all the risk drivers affecting an organization. We have found it both comprehensive and practical.

Of course, we may customize it to the specific needs of each organization, e.g. by using firm-specific terms for the seven risk types shown in The Dragonfly Risk Driver Framework. In some cases, we may unbundle one or more of the seven drivers where it is important for the specific organization. For example, the macro/environmental category may be unbundled into two – macro and regulatory – for an infrastructure industry player.

Linkages & Transformation of Risks

A risk incident in one risk driver category may cause a shortfall in a key parameter of one or more different risk types.

For example, with a hypothetical power company, a major flood could lead to the shutdown of a major substation. That could in turn lead to legal claims for damages by electronics manufacturers in an affected industrial park. How the power company handles the claims could lead to a reputational problem. In this example, a natural disaster risk creates an operational risk, which triggers legal risk, and results in reputational risk – showing that 4 different risk types can be linked.

Watching for linkages among risk drivers is as important as identifying the key risk types. This helps us understand why firms are sometimes surprised by less obvious sources of risk such as reputational hits. Many firms feel they are conservative and hence do not intentionally take reputational bets. However, as shown above, the linkages with other risk drivers can cause a reputational risk event.

Controllability Does *Not* Matter

It is intuitive to segment risk drivers into controllable and uncontrollable sources. Firms who do this, however, often wind up **not** quantifying uncontrollable risks.

The Dragonfly Approach shows that classifying a risk driver as controllable or uncontrollable is not only *not* a useful distinction, it could even be *dangerous*. For example, we may not be able to control natural disaster risk, and we may have limited influence on political conditions. But these are real and potentially large sources of risks affecting our goals. They must be quantified even if they are uncontrollable.

Therefore, to know our bets, we must identify *all* risk drivers, whether they *are controllable or not*. This is a caution we have had to raise to many client CEOs. Controllability is a useful concept *only* in evaluating options for managing risks. (For example, for non-controllable risks, we may rely on early warning indicators, contingency plans and insurance protection). We will discuss this further in Chapter 8.

Recap: Know Your Bets. You Are Always Taking Bets

CEOs need to ensure their executives are mindful **that they are taking bets** for every goal they pursue. First, they should use The Dragonfly Strategic Bets Framework to identify the bets underlying every goal. Then, they should use The Dragonfly Universe of Risk Drivers & Linkages to identify *all* risk drivers that affect the organization and its goals, and the potential linkages among them.

> " All goals involve uncertainty, which means that as a CEO you are always taking bets. Therefore, as CEO, you need to know what the bets are. "

Risk Insights from Chapter 2

Know Your Bets. You Are Always Taking Bets

1. As a CEO you are always taking bets — because all goals you set are uncertain.

2. The bets you take are the sources or causes of the risk or uncertainty in attaining your goals.

3. To understand the uncertainty inherent in your goals, you need to know what bets you are taking.

4. Therefore, to "know your bets" is a first step to effective risk management.

5. Dragonfly offers 2 templates — at 2 levels — for identifying your bets:

   a. The Dragonfly Strategic Bets Framework — an overarching tool to help you identify risk drivers quickly, by emphasizing that underlying every goal are 4 types of "bets":
      - Demand
      - Capabilities
      - Competition
      - Macro/Environment

   b. The Dragonfly Universe of Risk Drivers and Linkages — a comprehensive organization-wide tool to identify *all* the "bets" taken throughout the firm and their potential linkages.

CHAPTER 3

3

WHY ALL RISKS SHOULD BE QUANTIFIED

Many CEOs are unsure if they really need to quantify risk in their business. Some are told that only financial institutions really need to quantify risks. Others are advised that only "financial" risks can be quantified.

Our answer is **you MUST quantify ALL risks in your business**. As discussed in Chapter 2, we take risks, whether or not we acknowledge doing so, and even if we are unaware of the risks.

How can a CEO evaluate the amount and mix of risks? To do so, the risks must first be *quantified*.

Specifically, as a CEO, you need to be able to make the following critical risk determinations:

1. Whether the firm has the means to take the risks
2. Whether the risk taken is worth the potential earnings
3. Whether it is worth reducing the risk
4. Whether you can charge enough to take on more risk
5. What your risk appetite is
6. How much capital you need

In order to answer the above, it is necessary to quantify your risks. (See Exhibit 3.1).

Exhibit 3.1: All Risks *Must* Be Quantified

To Make CEO Risk Decisions Effectively

Strategic   **Operational**

Risk Capacity

Adequate Returns

How Much Risk

Risk Appetite   Capital Required   Pricing Required   Risk Reduction Attractive-ness

All Risks Must Be Quantified

We will show in this chapter that *all* firms need to quantify risk for the following reasons:

1. To Determine Whether Your Firm Has the Capacity to Take the Risks

The size of risks taken determines the potential volatility in a firm's earnings and valuation. It will also cause volatility in the firm's cash flow and therefore affect the amount of debt that it can handle. Hence, the amount of risks taken determines the level of capital a firm needs to maintain its credit rating, and ultimately to stay solvent.

Unless you can quantify the risks you are taking, you will not be able to determine:

1. If you have the capacity to take that level of risk;
2. How much equity and debt you need to secure; and
3. How much volatility in performance you can handle, taking your stakeholders' preferences into consideration.

Many firms today are unable to quantify some or all of the risks they are taking. Hence, discussions and decisions about risk are often unsatisfactory, contentious and inconclusive.

The CEO may feel that the risk of a major investment is acceptable, while an independent director may believe the risk is too high. Without quantification, it is difficult to sort that out. Both views could be correct, as there is no uniform way of calibrating the risk without a quantification methodology. There is also no robust way to measure how much of the firm's capacity to take risk would be used in that investment.

2. To Determine Whether the Risk Taken Is Worth the Potential Earnings

At first blush, it seems easy to estimate potential returns. Most of us put a lot of effort into projecting the numerator, i.e. the cash flow or earnings. But we take a more expedient approach in calculating the denominator, i.e. how much capital we need. Often we simply use peer comparables.

Without quantifying the risks required to generate the potential cash flow or earnings, we cannot calculate the amount of capital required. This means we cannot assess if the potential earnings are worth the amount of risk taken.

3. To Determine Whether It is Worth Reducing the Risk

When the risk is quantified, you can evaluate the net impact of risk transfer or reduction. You can then see if the reduction in risk is worth paying for. There is typically a direct cost for the risk reduction transaction. In addition, there may be a decrease in revenues as you are now taking on less risk. However, the capital required is also lower since the risk has been reduced. You need to determine if the return on capital is improved if you reduce the risk.

4. To Determine Whether You Can Charge Enough for the Risks You Take

Customers often look for lower risk solutions, such as fixed price long-term maintenance contracts.

For example, imagine you are an independent MRO (maintenance, repair, overhaul) provider for airlines. An airline customer is asking for a 5-year fixed rate contract for the maintenance of its fleet of aircraft. You offer a competitive $125/flight hour fixed for 5 years, when the prevailing spot rate for this year's maintenance is $110/flight hour. Your customer is willing to pay this $15/flight hour premium to lock in his costs for 5 years. In such a case, you would be taking on the risk of the spot rate rising. This is the risk that the customer does not want to bear.

As CEO, you know you are taking the risk that the $15/flight hour premium might not be adequate to cover the possibility of equipment reliability, labor and material costs turning out worse than expected over the next 5 years.

To be able to price the long term fixed rate contract, you need to quantify the risks incurred. You can then figure out if you can charge enough for the risks taken and still offer a price that is attractive to the customer.

5. To Determine Your Risk Appetite

Risk appetite is one of the top 5 issues that CEOs raise with Dragonfly.

How much risk should I take? How do I decide if I am conservative enough? Or am I too risk averse? How do I allocate scarce capital across all the compelling ideas my business lines present to me?

The information you need to answer this set of questions are the level and mix of risks – which means you must quantify your risks.

Whether your risk appetite is conservative or not depends on the amount of risk you take versus the risk capacity you have. To allocate capital among the business lines, you need to know the appropriate amount of capital each business line requires, given the risks they have to take on – which again means that you need to quantify the risks each business line would be taking.

6. To Determine How Much Capital You Need

Related to the risk appetite decision is the question of how much capital the firm needs. That depends primarily on how much risk you need to take – which is driven by the value, level and nature of the business you want to do. Again, you need to quantify risks to be able to accurately determine the amount of capital you need.

Although the amount of risk taken should account for most of the capital the firm needs, there are a few other considerations, for example, the CEO may need to consider additional capital for possible near-term growth initiatives such as acquisitions, as well as growth in working capital.

Recap: Why All Risks Should Be Quantified

For some firms, especially financial institutions, risk quantification is required by regulation and/or by credit rating agencies. However, we believe we have shown in this chapter that even without external requirements, all CEOs have compelling reasons to quantify their firm's risks, i.e. to determine:

- The firm's capacity for taking risk
- Whether potential earnings justify the risks taken
- Whether risk reduction is useful
- Whether customers pay enough for risk absorbed by your firm
- What the firm's risk appetite should be
- How much capital the firm needs

Unfortunately, some CEOs have been advised erroneously that not all risks can be quantified. The next chapter will discuss why *all* risks *can* be quantified and The Dragonfly Approach for doing so.

Risk Insights from Chapter 3

Why All Risks Should Be Quantified

1. Your organization takes risks, whether you acknowledge it or not, and even if you are unaware of the risks.

2. But it is impossible to evaluate and decide on risks properly if you do not quantify them.

3. Further, as CEO, you need to quantify risks in order to make the following critical determinations:

   a. Whether the firm has the means to take the risks;
   b. Whether the risk taken is worth the potential earnings;
   c. Whether it is worth reducing the risk;
   d. Whether you can charge enough to take on more risk;
   e. What your risk appetite is; and
   f. How much capital you need.

4. Hence, as CEO you need to quantify the risk your firm takes, even if you are not required to do so by regulators and/or ratings agencies.

CHAPTER 4

ALL RISKS CAN BE QUANTIFIED

Most CEOs intuitively feel that all risks *should* be quantified. However, many CEOs have doubts that all risks *can* be quantified. Unfortunately, many of their risk managers and advisors also feel similarly constrained. Dragonfly will show in this chapter that this is a misconception – a serious one for CEOs. We will then show you why **all risks *can* be quantified**.

We will lay out **The Dragonfly Risk Quantification Framework** that shows:

1. Where risks come from;
2. What drives the nature and size of all risks; and
3. The process for quantifying any and all risks.

1. Where Risks Come From

All goals depend on an operating configuration of inputs and processes. Think of the firm as a "factory" run by a CEO to attain the firm's goals.

The "factory" is an operating configuration consisting of several processes (e.g. equipment, information, technology and locations) and various inputs (e.g. people, materials, data). There are also linkages and interdependencies among the processes, and also between inputs and the processes. (See Exhibit 4.1).

66 The risk distribution of any goal is determined by the exposure, sensitivity and size of shock of each applicable risk driver. 99

Exhibit 4.1: Understand Where Risks Come From

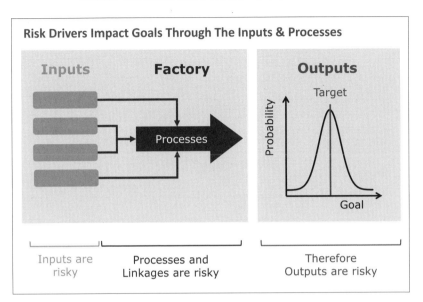

Most inputs exhibit some uncertainty (i.e. they are not guaranteed). There are also sources of uncertainties in the operating processes, as well as in the linkages. In Chapter 2, "Know Your Bets", we named these various sources of uncertainty "risk drivers".

We can use Exhibit 2.3 (The Dragonfly Universe of Risk Drivers and Linkages) as a checklist for identifying the specific risk types applicable to your "factory". (See Exhibit 4.1 and the various inputs, processes and linkages above). Once the applicable risk drivers have been identified, we move on to Step 2 below – examining the nature and size of each risk.

2. What Drives the Nature and Size of Risk

The risk of any goal is impacted by every risk driver to which the goal is exposed. The risk distribution – shape and size – is determined by three components:

    a. Exposure
    b. Sensitivity
    c. Size of Shock

The next section describes how each of the 3 components drives the nature or size of risk, i.e. the risk distribution. (See Exhibit 4.2).

Exhibit 4.2: Drivers of Shape and Size of Risk

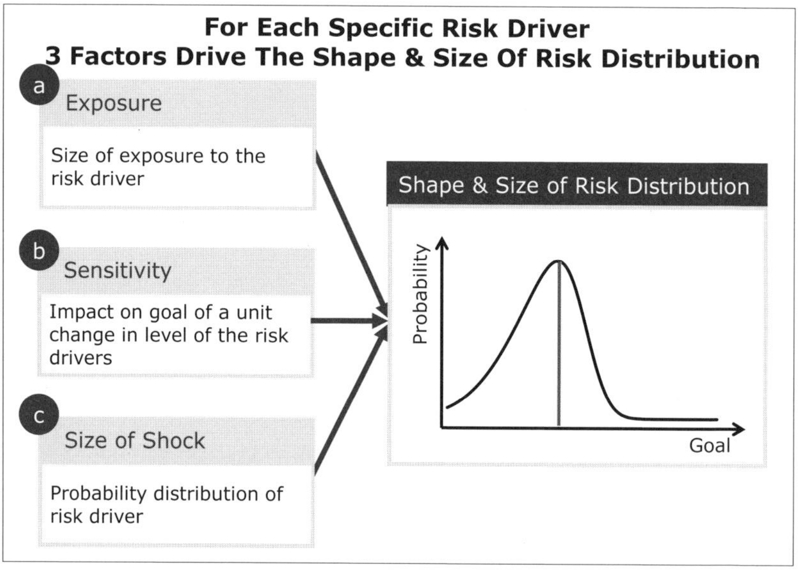

For Each Specific Risk Driver
3 Factors Drive The Shape & Size Of Risk Distribution

a Exposure

Size of exposure to the risk driver

b Sensitivity

Impact on goal of a unit change in level of the risk drivers

c Size of Shock

Probability distribution of risk driver

Shape & Size of Risk Distribution

Probability

Goal

a. Exposure

This is easy to understand – the larger the exposure to the risk driver, the larger the potential risk impact. Exposures are also straightforward in that they are easy to identify and quantify. The data is objective, factual and usually already recorded somewhere in the organization.

b. Sensitivity

This is also intuitive – a goal may be more sensitive to one risk driver than another. For example, airline earnings are more sensitive to fuel price changes than to food costs.

Sensitivities, like exposures, are also objective, factual and non-controversial. However, some business models and some goals involve complicated operational processes. In these cases, a goal may have a non-linear and/or asymmetric relationship with the risk driver, making the sensitivity unintuitive and/or hard to visualize. Further, the sensitivity may not be a constant value; depending on the business model, the sensitivity may be different at different levels of the risk driver.

Even so, the sensitivity is still neither controversial nor subjective. It just requires some modeling or analysis to figure out.

c. Size of Shock

The third component that determines the nature and size of risk is the potential size of the "shock" for the risk driver. The shock is how adverse the level of the risk driver could turn out to be, compared to the target (or expected) level.

For example, if fuel price is the risk driver, and the expected level is, say, $50/barrel, then the size of shock could be $15 (i.e. fuel price could be $15 higher, reaching $65/barrel).

Since risk covers all the levels that a risk driver could turn out to be that is different from the target, what we need to assess is the potential distribution of different levels of the risk driver, or the probability of each possible level of shock. Exhibit 4.3 shows the different shapes of risk distributions that are possible.

Exhibit 4.3: Shapes of Risk Distributions

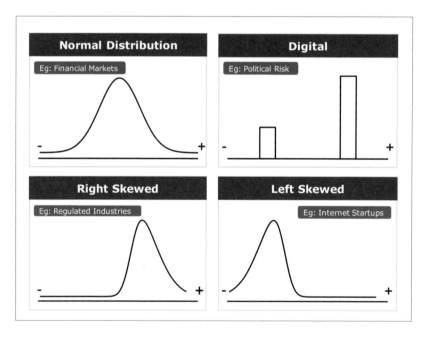

Unfortunately, this third component is subjective, unlike the other two components (exposure, sensitivity). We have to use available knowledge and our best judgment to determine the distribution of the risk driver.

Looking at lots of historical experience helps. It is critical to understand the structural conditions that were present and to assess if future conditions could be similar. It is also useful to look at similar drivers in other industries, including how structural conditions persist or change in other sectors.

The judgment and associated effort and skill required for this aspect of risk quantification may make some CEOs uncomfortable at first. But when we point out that making decisions and judgment calls with incomplete information and/or under uncertainty is precisely what CEOs do, they begin to accept the reality of risk quantification.

We also point out that risk quantification is not the same as forecasting. We do not have to guess correctly the actual resultant level of the risk driver. Rather, we are trying to assess and incorporate the full range of possible outcomes, as well as their associated probabilities. Much less precision is required. It is a doable task. With effort and skill, it is a critical task that can be done satisfactorily and consistently.

Illustration of Risk Quantification

Let's re-use our hypothetical budget airline to illustrate The Dragonfly Risk Quantification Framework. See Exhibit 4.4 below.

Exhibit 4.4: Example of Risk Quantification

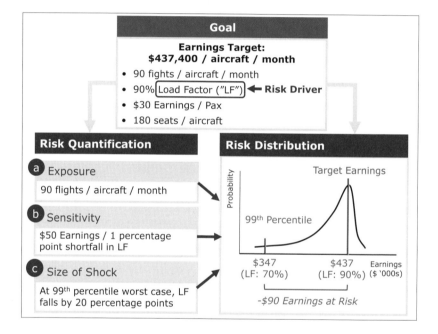

The goal is earnings and the risk driver is the load factor, a result of passenger demand. We are quantifying the risk of earnings shortfall due to volatility in the load factor (or passenger demand).

The 3 components of risk quantification:

a. Exposure: the number of flights per aircraft per month – which in our example is 90.
b. Sensitivity: calculated based on the revenue and cost dynamics, at $50 per 1 percentage point shortfall in load factor attained.
c. Shock: at the 99th percentile worst case, the load factor would drop to 70%. This is a shortfall of 20 percentage points from the target load factor of 90%.

The size of risk, at the 99th percentile downside in load factor, is:

- Exposure × Sensitivity × Shock
- 90 flights/month × $50 per load factor point × 20 point drop in load factor
- Risk: $90,000/month
- Target earnings: $437,400/aircraft/month
- (3 flights/days × 30 days/month × 90% load factor × 180 seats/aircraft) × $30 earnings/pax
- Risk can also be shown as a 21% shortfall in target earnings ($90,000÷$437,400)

The Dragonfly Risk Quantification Process

Using The Dragonfly Risk Quantification Framework, we have shown why all risks *can* be quantified:

- We know where risks come from (by using The Dragonfly Strategic Bets Framework and The Dragonfly Universe of Risk Drivers and Linkages from Chapter 2)
- We know the 3 components that drive the size of risk and the shape of the risk distribution – Exposure, Sensitivity, and Shock

This next section will lay out **The Dragonfly Risk Quantification Process** for any risk driver, for any firm, in any sector. (See Exhibit 4.5 below).

Exhibit 4.5: The Dragonfly Risk Quantification Process

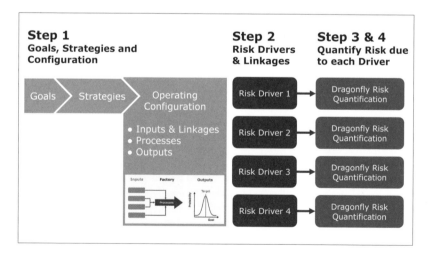

Step 1 Understand the goals and strategy of the firm and lay out the operating configuration – goals, strategy, operating processes, inputs and linkages.

Step 2 Identify the risk drivers and linkages among the drivers.

Step 3 For each risk driver:
- Quantify the exposure;
- Model the sensitivity of the goal(s) to changes in the risk driver;
- Identify the probability distribution of different levels of shock (downside and upside) for the risk driver; and
- Compute the risk distribution of the possible outcomes of the goal(s) for the risk driver.

Step 4 Repeat Step 3 for every risk driver relevant to the goal(s) whose riskiness we are evaluating.

"Reputational, political, strategic and operational risks are commonly found to be difficult to handle and, as a result, assumed to be unquantifiable. "

Why the Misconception that Some Risks Cannot Be Quantified

Many CEOs are concerned that some risks cannot be quantified. Dragonfly will show in this section that it is a misconception caused by 4 common problems. (See Exhibit 4.6 below).

Exhibit 4.6: All Risks *Can* Be Quantified

Common Misconception That Some Risks Are Unquantifiable But Dragonfly Shows That All Risks *Can* Be Quantified

Examples of "Unquantifiable Risks"

- Reputational Risk
- Political Risk
- Operational Risk
- Non – Financial Risk

Underlying Problems

- Some risk types are "hard to quantify"
- One or more quantifiable steps not done
- Goals stated qualitatively
- Non-financial goals assumed to be qualitative

Dragonfly Approach

1. Apply The Dragonfly Risk Quantification Framework
2. Complete the quantification steps
3. Specify goals; restate quantitatively if necessary

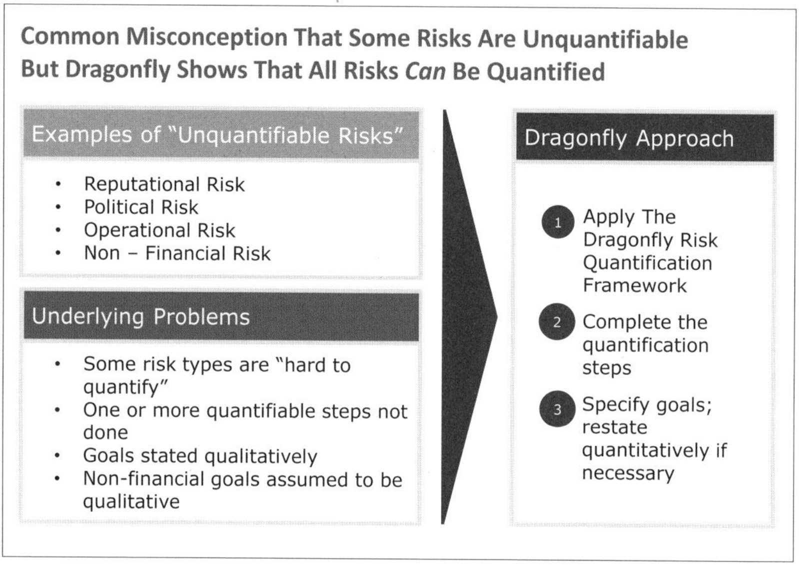

1. Hard-to-Quantify Risk Types

Some risk types are more challenging to understand and evaluate. Reputational, political, strategic and operational risks are commonly found to be difficult to handle and, as a result, assumed to be unquantifiable. This is a serious misconception.

48

For example, most firms do not purposely decide to take a certain level of reputational risk. Further, most do not see a direct link between the product or typical customer decisions and reputational risk. So this source of risk is not even identified, never mind quantified.

Dragonfly, however, believes that reputational risk *can* be understood and quantified. To do so, we must lay out the operating model and look for linkages among risk drivers. For example, operational risk could lead to reputational risk, depending on customer expectations and on how customers view the firm's handling of the impact of reputational setbacks.

In some cases, it might be the risk from natural disasters that causes an operational failure, which then creates a legal situation. Depending on how the legal situation is handled (again from the perspective of the customer, relative to their expectations), you might end up with a reputational setback.

The preceding examples show how easy it is to miss identifying a risk driver, especially if it is dependent on or linked to another risk type, or if it arises from a chain of risk incidents. This is a primary reason why some risks are hard to quantify. But it does not mean they *cannot* be quantified.

2. Quantification Steps Not Done

Using The Dragonfly Risk Quantification Framework, we can see that in some cases, the effort of identifying the size of exposures and modeling the sensitivities has not been made. Also, as mentioned earlier in this chapter, the risk sensitivities may not be intuitive and may be impossible to visualize without specific modeling work. Even if the analysts are aware of operational risk, for example, they would not be able to quantify its impact if they do not model the risk sensitivity properly.

As many risk analysts are intimidated by the degree of domain knowledge required, as well as the intricate nature of many operational processes, they often do not undertake the work required by The Dragonfly Risk Quantification Framework.

3. When Goals are Qualitative

Another reason for the misconception that some risks cannot be quantified is that the underlying goals are stated qualitatively. For example, a top goal of the Red Cross might be to increase community participation. At first blush, this looks like a qualitative goal. However, with a bit more effort the goal can be stated quantitatively, such as percentage growth in the number of volunteers. Hence both the goal and the risk metric used can be stated quantitatively.

In practice, we have found that even goals that are qualitative can be reviewed and restated quantitatively. Therefore, we believe that all risks can be quantified.

4. Even Non-Financial Goals are Quantifiable

Every organization has some goals that are non-financial. However, there is a common misconception that only financial risks are quantifiable. This is partly because risk management was first developed and used for financial institutions.

In fact, non-financial goals can be quantified. As discussed in Chapter 1, risk metrics can be derived from these non-financial goals and used to quantify the risks.

For example, a development agency's goal is to create manufacturing jobs – not a financial goal, but certainly a quantitative goal. Hence, if we understand and specify the goal(s) and risk metric(s), we would realize that the risk impact is quantitative.

To recap, the reasons for the common misconception that some risks cannot be quantified are:

1. Some risk drivers are more challenging to quantify.
2. The analyst does not use a robust framework for identifying where those risks come from and how the impact can be quantified.
3. The goals are stated qualitatively.
4. The goals are non-financial goals, coupled with the common misconception that only financial risks are quantifiable.

Recap: All Risks Can Be Quantified

This chapter shows CEOs why all risks can be quantified. We discussed The Dragonfly Risk Quantification Framework that shows:

- Where risks come from
- What drives the nature and size of risk

We also laid out The Dragonfly Risk Quantification Process.

Finally, we identified the reasons for the common misconception that some risks cannot be quantified. The Dragonfly Risk Quantification Framework and Process have been developed and used successfully by the authors across all risk types and many industries/sectors for 25+ years.

66 There is a common misconception that only financial risks are quantifiable. This is partly because risk management was first developed and used for financial institutions. 99

Risk Insights from Chapter 4

All Risks Can Be Quantified

1. Although most CEOs understand the need to quantify risks, many doubt that all risks can be quantified.

2. All risks can indeed be quantified.

3. Dragonfly has developed a Risk Quantification Framework that shows:

   a. Where risks come from; and
   b. What drives the nature and size of risk.

4. For each risk driver we show that the nature and size of risk are driven by:

   a. Exposure
   b. Sensitivity
   c. Size of shock

5. This chapter also demonstrates The Dragonfly Risk Quantification Process:

   a. Lay out goals, strategy, operating processes;
   b. Identify risk drivers and linkages; and
   c. For each risk driver, perform risk quantification.

6. Unfortunately, there is a common misconception that some risks cannot be quantified.

7. We use The Dragonfly Risk Quantification Framework and Process to explain the causes of the misconception:

   a. Some risk types are harder to understand, evaluate and quantify;

   b. Some quantification steps are not performed, usually due to the lack of understanding and know-how;

   c. Underlying goals are stated qualitatively;

   d. Misconception that non-financial goals are not quantitative.

CHAPTER 5

5

HOW TO QUANTIFY & EVALUATE STRATEGIC RISK

Making decisions on strategy and strategic investments are among the most critical roles for CEOs. They know that these decisions are high impact and that the options available are all risky.

In our work, we have seen strategy and investment papers submitted to boards of directors in companies worldwide and across many sectors. In almost all the papers we see two types of risk analysis:

1. 3-scenario approach: most likely, optimistic, pessimistic
2. List of top risks and mitigation plans

Most CEOs and board directors intuitively feel that the typical risk evaluation, while important, is incomplete and insufficient. This is because risk is not properly quantified, if at all.

Many CEOs are told that strategic risk cannot be quantified. Some are shown pseudo-quantitative approaches like risk scoring. These typically use a scale of 1 to 5 for severity, multiplied by an identical scale for likelihood; the risk scores therefore range from 1 to 25.

This is frustrating for CEOs as they understand that without proper quantification, they cannot evaluate strategic risk satisfactorily. Fortunately, the notion that strategic risk cannot be quantified is a misconception, albeit a widespread one. **Dragonfly has developed a robust methodology for quantifying and evaluating strategic risk**. We do *not* use a scoring approach, as it is unreliable at best and spurious at worst. Instead, we quantify strategic risk using the same metrics in which the firm's goals are stated.

In Chapter 4, we showed why all risks *can* be quantified. In this chapter, we will show how those principles can be applied to strategic risks, using **The Dragonfly Strategic Risk Quantification Process**.

> 66 Most CEOs and board directors intuitively feel that the typical risk evaluation, while important, is incomplete and insufficient. This is because risk is not properly quantified, if at all. 99

Exhibit 5.1: The Dragonfly Strategic Risk Quantification Process

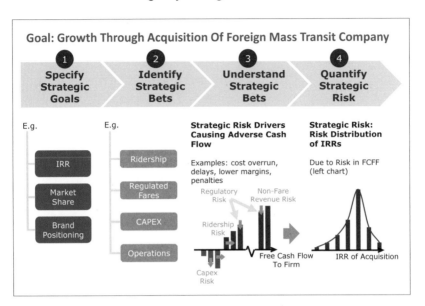

1. Specify Your Strategic Goals

Strategic decisions typically come with financial goals such as IRRs, earnings growth and valuation. Of course, there may also be some non-financial goals such as competitive advantage, market share, and brand positioning. As you may recall from Chapter 1, the first step in risk quantification is to specify your goals.

We will illustrate The Dragonfly Strategic Risk Quantification Process with an example of a growth strategy based on an acquisition of a mass transit company (rail, buses, taxis) in a foreign country. The goals are growth in earnings and a target hurdle rate or IRR of 13%.

2. Identify the Strategic Bets

Next we identify the bets taken to pursue the goal(s) for which this strategy is chosen, i.e. the "strategic bets".

Exhibit 5.2: Strategic Risk Bets

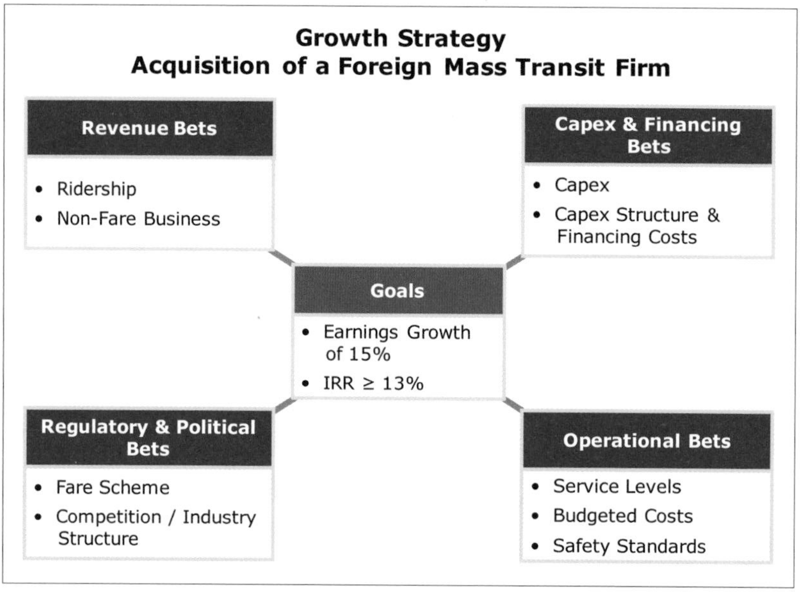

Growth Strategy
Acquisition of a Foreign Mass Transit Firm

Revenue Bets		Capex & Financing Bets
• Ridership • Non-Fare Business		• Capex • Capex Structure & Financing Costs

Goals

- Earnings Growth of 15%
- IRR ≥ 13%

Regulatory & Political Bets		Operational Bets
• Fare Scheme • Competition / Industry Structure		• Service Levels • Budgeted Costs • Safety Standards

For our hypothetical acquisition of a mass transit firm, we've identified the strategic bets as:

a. Revenue Bets
   i. Average daily ridership (the fare-based business)
   ii. Non-fare business (mostly rentals of transit station retail space and advertising)

b. <u>Capex and Financing Bets</u>
  i. Capex for trains, buses, taxis and related equipment
  ii. Capital structure and financing costs

c. <u>Operational Bets</u>
  i. Ability to meet target service levels at budgeted costs (e.g. frequency of trains, maximum allowed service interruptions)
  ii. Safety standards

d. <u>Regulatory and Political Bets</u>
  i. Fare / Pricing regime
  ii. Competition / Industry structure

3. Understand the Strategic Bets

We need to understand the risk profile of each of these bets. To do so, we research and analyze how the structural and operating conditions could affect the behavior of each strategic driver. It requires empirical analysis of historical data. It may also require the building of a simulation model to generate a full range of possible outcomes given different inputs.

   " The Dragonfly Strategic Risk Quantification Process is more powerful than the traditional methodology using 3 scenarios to depict risk. "

Exhibit 5.3 below illustrates the risk distributions applicable to our example.

Exhibit 5.3: Analyze & Evaluate Risk Drivers

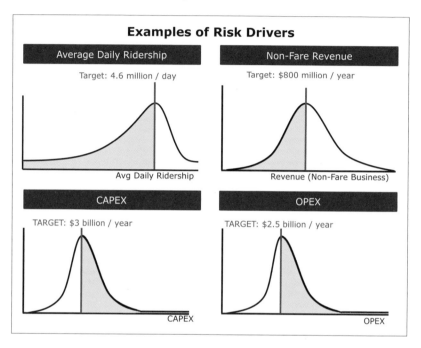

4. Quantify Strategic Risk

The next step is to run the cash flow model using the risk distribution of each strategic bet (or risk driver) where relevant.

The combined impact of all the risk drivers is the output of the Dragonfly Strategic Risk Quantification Process (Exhibit 5.1). For our transit company acquisition example, it would be the probability distribution of returns (IRR). The distribution shows the risk of the strategy in a quantitative way, e.g. the different levels of IRRs that the acquisition might achieve, with their respective probabilities.

Let's explore the nature of the strategic risk, i.e. the uncertainty in the IRR attainable. The risks of the underlying strategic bets – such as ridership, service levels attainable – create the potential volatility in the cash flows attained. Because the cash flow is risky, the IRR goal is risky. (See Exhibit 5.4 below).

Exhibit 5.4: Impact Of Risk Drivers On Cash Flow & IRRs

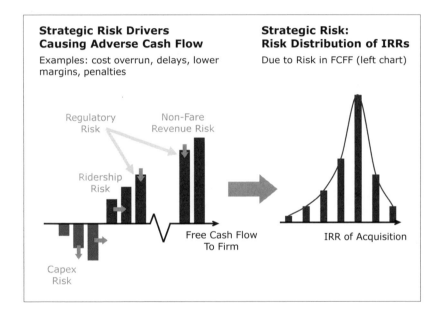

Strategic Risk Drivers Causing Adverse Cash Flow

Examples: cost overrun, delays, lower margins, penalties

Strategic Risk: Risk Distribution of IRRs

Due to Risk in FCFF (left chart)

Regulatory Risk · Non-Fare Revenue Risk · Ridership Risk · Capex Risk · Free Cash Flow To Firm · IRR of Acquisition

Evaluating Strategy Risk: Dragonfly vs Traditional Method

The preceding section demonstrates The Dragonfly Strategic Risk Quantification Process. Next, we will discuss how it is a more powerful way to evaluate strategic decisions than the traditional method of using 3 scenarios to depict risk (most likely, optimistic & pessimistic cases).

a. Full Distribution of Risk

Exhibit 5.5 compares both approaches.

The Dragonfly Strategic Risk Quantification Process gives you the complete risk distribution – all the possible IRRs with the respective probabilities.

The traditional approach shows only 3 of the possible IRRs. It does not explicitly state the respective probabilities. There is a chance that the 3 scenarios are skewed (e.g. all 3 can be too optimistic, as you can see from the left chart).

Exhibit 5.5: Evaluate the Full Distribution of Possible IRRs, Instead of Using Typical Three-Scenario Metric

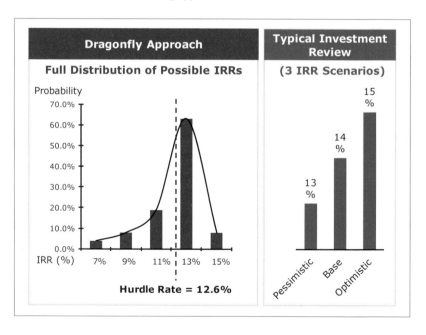

b. <u>Improve Your Risk-Return Profile</u>

In addition, since The Dragonfly Strategic Risk Quantification Process links the underlying strategic drivers to the cash flow, we can use the model to evaluate deal structure or business model configuration options, in order to determine how a more acceptable risk-return profile (which in our example would be a more attractive IRR distribution) might be possible. (See Exhibit 5.6 below)

Exhibit 5.6: Improving Your Risk-Return Profile

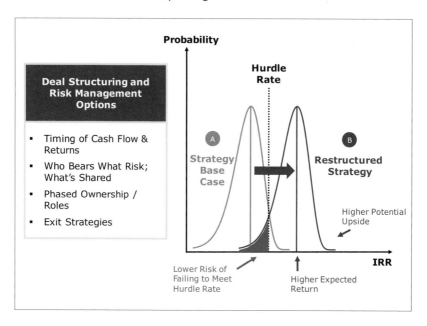

c. <u>Dragonfly Approach Improves Upon Conventional Hurdle Rate Methodology</u>

The Dragonfly Strategic Risk Quantification Process also fundamentally improves upon the typical way firms account for risk when evaluating investments.

The "textbook" approach is to add risk premia to the base hurdle rate (which is itself estimated using CAPM and/or industry comparables). In practice, we have seen 3 to 6 percentage points being added to the base hurdle rate for acquisitions and infrastructure investments, for instance.

Dragonfly believes that this conventional approach is crude. It could work for *true* portfolio investments (like bond or equity portfolios), but it is too simplistic for the strategy decisions or strategic investments that most CEOs have to deal with. These decisions are normally not part of a large enough set of deals, so it *cannot* be treated statistically as a portfolio.

The conventional approach works for asset management portfolios, for which the methodology was originally developed. Most CEOs however, evaluate only a handful of very large and dissimilar deals. Therefore, the conventional portfolio approach does *not* work well universally.

Furthermore, in the low interest rate environment (for most countries) of the last 10 years, many CEOs intuitively noticed that the risk premium used in their hurdle rates were too high compared with the level of the market.

The Dragonfly Strategic Risk Quantification Process **treats risk in 2 separate, though related, ways**:

i. The **beta risk** is handled using CAPM (in line with finance theory).

ii. The **cash flow risk** is quantified using The Dragonfly Strategic Risk Quantification Process described in this chapter. The riskiness is used to determine the appropriate capital structure. The higher the risk, the higher the equity required for the target credit rating (or default probability). (See Exhibit 5.7 below)

Exhibit 5.7: Risk Quantification & Capital Structure

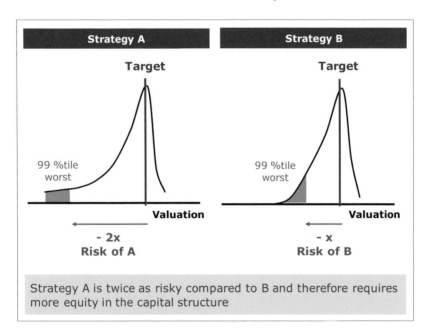

Our approach therefore accounts for the two types of risks separately – the beta risk (as in i. above), and the cash flow or default / solvency risk (as in ii. above). It is more accurate and robust than the blunt approach of adding a risk premium of 100-200 basis points for each risk driver. It is also more defensible.

d. Determines the Appropriate Capital Structure
Finally, The Dragonfly Strategic Risk Quantification Process solves the problem of figuring out what the capital structure (or appropriate gearing) should be, given the riskiness of the strategy or investment. In Exhibit 5.7 above, Strategy A requires twice the amount of equity capital than Strategy B.

Recap: How to Quantify & Evaluate Strategic Risk

To recap, The Dragonfly Strategic Risk Quantification Process is more powerful than conventional practice because it:

a. Shows the full distribution of risk;
b. Helps improve the risk-return profile;
c. Improves upon conventional hurdle rate methodology; and
d. Helps make better capital structure decisions.

Although The Dragonfly Approach requires more data and analysis than conventional practice, the additional effort is justified because strategy and strategic investment decisions are large enough and sufficiently risky.

> 66 The Dragonfly Strategic Risk Quantification Process gives you the complete risk distribution -- all the possible IRRs with their respective probabilities. 99

Risk Insights from Chapter 5

How to Quantify and Evaluate Strategic Risk

1. Making strategy and investment decisions is where a CEO directly decides on risks (taken or not taken).

2. Many CEOs have been advised erroneously that strategic risk cannot be quantified.

3. The conventional approach for handling risk in strategic investments uses scoring methods and adds risk premia to hurdle rates.

4. Although risk scoring is attractive because it is easy to use, it is a blunt and inadequate approach.

5. Instead of scoring, Dragonfly uses a robust risk quantification methodology for evaluating strategic risk decisions – The Dragonfly Strategic Risk Quantification Process:

   a. Specify your goals;
   b. Identify the strategic bets;
   c. Understand the bets;
   d. Quantify impact of strategic risk (on your own goals);
   e. Show full risk distribution instead of the typical 3-scenario outcomes; and
   f. Review structuring options to modify risk-return profile (if desired).

6. The Dragonfly Strategic Risk Quantification Process is more powerful than conventional practice because it:

a. Shows the full distribution of risk;

b. Helps improve the risk-return profile;

c. Improves upon conventional hurdle rate methodology; and

d. Helps make better capital structure decisions.

CHAPTER 6

6

DECIDING YOUR RISK APPETITE

The three most important risk decisions a board of directors has to make are:

1. What is the organization's risk appetite?
2. Does it have the financial capacity to take that level and mix of risks?
3. Do the CEO and organization have risk management capabilities adequate for its risk appetite?

Risk appetite is the level and mix of risks you decide to take on. Your firm's strategy, business plan, budget and performance targets determine the level and mix of risks you will need. You and your organization have a risk appetite, whether you know it or not, and whether you quantify your risks or not.

Although most CEOs and boards of directors are aware of the need to decide on the firm's risk appetite, few organizations today are able to do so. Many are unable to fully quantify their risks. Others are unsure of the approach for deciding their risk appetite. This is because CEOs and boards of directors often lack the necessary data or tools.

The Dragonfly Risk Appetite Framework

Our approach to making decisions on risk appetite starts with three *quantitative* assessments (See Exhibit 6.1 next page):

1. Figuring out your recent or current level and mix of risks. This may be called your *default* or *current* risk appetite, especially if it was not the result of an explicit decision-making process.
2. Determining the risks implied by the strategy, business plan and operating budget you have chosen for the next period. This is essentially your *target* risk appetite.
3. Understanding what your resources, capital and stakeholder expectations are, and how these factors constrain your risk appetite. These are your risk appetite *constraints*.

Exhibit 6.1: The Dragonfly Risk Appetite Framework
- 3 Quantitative Assessments

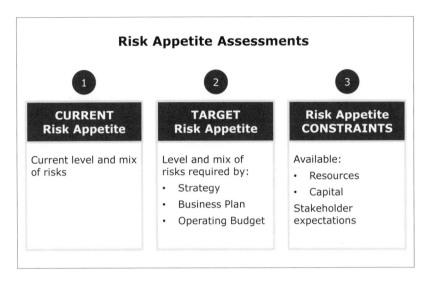

With the answers from the three aforementioned assessments, you can work out what your *desired* risk appetite is.

You can start with a "top-down" approach: Given your resource constraints and stakeholder concerns, what is the maximum risk appetite you can afford?

Or, you can use a "bottom-up" approach: Quantify the risk appetite required to support the aggregate of the operating budgets of all your business lines.

Whether you start top-down or bottom-up, the next step is to iterate between the two, using your current risk appetite as a baseline. Ultimately, the risk appetite decision is a judgment call – it is an "art", in that there is no "right number".

Exhibit 6.2: The Dragonfly Risk Appetite Framework
– An Iterative Decision Process

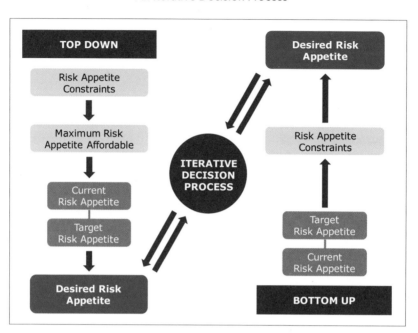

Deciding the risk appetite is partly the prerogative of the CEO. It should be based on his feel for the capabilities of the organization, his outlook of the macro-environment, and his "stomach" for taking on the level and mix of risks.

To be effective, we believe that a CEO should be well-informed with risk data and analytics (the "science") as he goes about making the judgment call and deciding on the risk appetite (the "art"). The Dragonfly Approach provides the data, tools and discipline – the "science" to support the CEO in the "art" of risk management. A key component of the "science" is **The Dragonfly Risk Dashboard**.

The Dragonfly Risk Dashboard

We have developed an enterprise-wide risk dashboard for our clients, to capture quantitatively, the complete set of risks taken by the firm. It shows the amount of risk taken by risk driver (represented by the columns in the Dashboard).

It also shows the risk taken by department (the rows in the Dashboard). Every single responsibility center is covered – product line, business line and function.

Exhibit 6.3: The Dragonfly Risk Dashboard

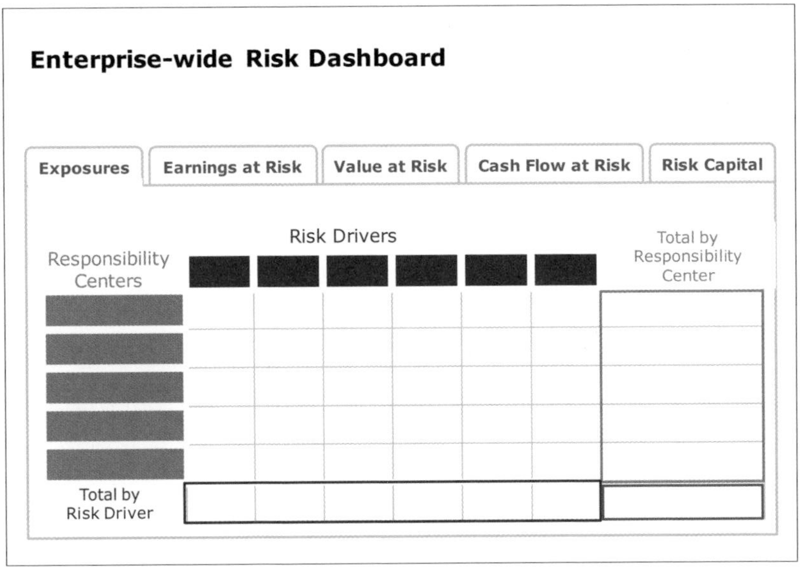

The key principle underlying the structure of the Dashboard is that *all* risks must be included. That is what we mean by "enterprise-wide". By structuring the Dashboard, as outlined above, we provide a disciplined regime to identify, capture and quantify *all* risks, wherever they are taken in the enterprise.

We can fill in the Dashboard in any one of the following ways, each being a separate and complete view of the firm's risks quantified as:

1. Exposures
2. Earnings at Risk
3. Value at Risk
4. Cash Flow at Risk
5. Risk Capital
6. Other Performance Metrics

Once compiled, The Dragonfly Risk Dashboard provides the CEO with the facts/information on:

1. *Who* is taking *what* bets, i.e. the level and mix of risks by risk driver;
2. The total amount of risk each organizational unit is taking, segmented by risk driver or risk type, and
3. The total amount of risk the organization is taking in *each* risk driver (i.e. each risk type).

The Dragonfly Risk Dashboard thus provides the CEO with comprehensive risk information – on both the *current* portfolio as well as the potential or *planned* portfolio – to make the decision on risk appetite.

Strategy, Budget and Risk Implications

All organizations have annual strategic planning and budgeting processes. However, in our experience, very few firms have evaluated and quantified the risk implications of their strategy and operating budget decisions.

As discussed in chapters 2 and 5, an organization's strategy sets the overarching "bets". These bets are operationalized in the budget, in resource allocation and performance targets. The exposures to these bets (or risk drivers) determine the amount and mix of risks the organization will be taking. Also, as emphasized in Chapter 2, the firm will be taking these bets even if it is unaware that it is doing so.

Therefore, any organization that desires to improve its resource and capital allocation process must incorporate risk quantification in its strategy and budgeting exercise.

The Dragonfly Risk Dashboard provides the framework, the data and the discipline for the risk quantification and evaluation process.

Resource Constraints & Stakeholder Concerns

All organizations face constraints in the resources to which they have access. Stakeholders have desired goals and targets. They also have concerns and limits. These factors will determine the risk appetite that the board of directors will be comfortable with and approve.

The Risk Dashboard is a tool that facilitates the articulation, evaluation and decision-making on whether the level and mix of risks fit within the organization's resource constraints and stakeholder concerns.

Essential Versions of the Risk Dashboard

For an organization that has a risk quantification process, the Risk Dashboard should be compiled in several versions:

- Historical portfolio of risks taken
- Prospective portfolio of risks (given the strategy & operating budget)
- Approved portfolio of risks (or the limits set for levels and mix of risks)
- Current portfolio of risks taken (today's, this week's or this month's, as appropriate)

66 To be effective, we believe that a CEO should be well-informed with risk data and analytics (the "science") as he goes about making the judgment call and deciding on the risk appetite (the "art"). 99

Deciding Your Risk Appetite – The Dragonfly Philosophy

We believe that the most satisfactory way to decide on risk appetite is to **have a mindset of minimizing *surprises*, not minimizing *risks*** (See Exhibit 6.4 below).

This means we first look at our goals and targets, as well as the strategy and operating budget that we have selected to attain our objectives. Next, we identify the "bets" that we will be taking and quantify the level and mix of risks that these "bets" bring with them. We analyze what resources are required, what potential volatility in performance we might face, then quantify the potential downside from our targets that we might suffer.

Exhibit 6.4: The Dragonfly Risk Philosophy
-- Minimizing Surprises

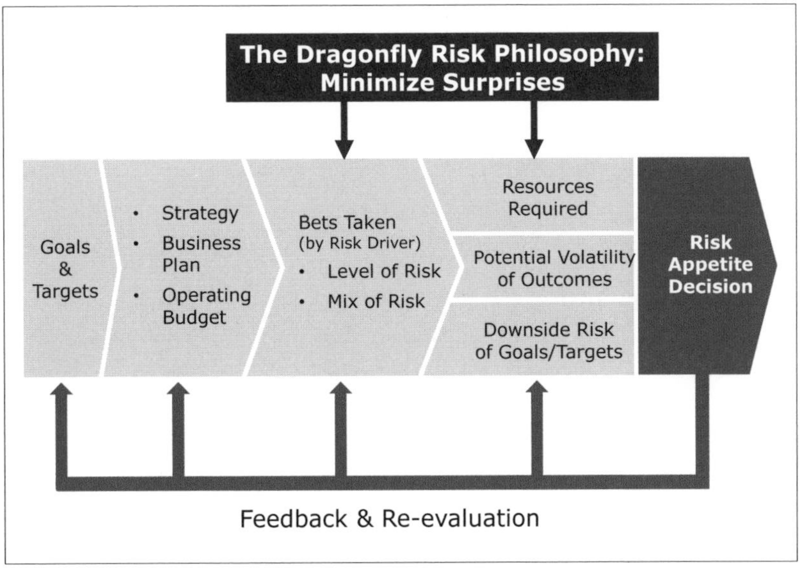

This is not a pessimistic orientation. It does not suggest that we will not attain our goals. In fact, we might even exceed our targets. What this means is that we go in knowing what the risks are, what could go wrong and how bad it could be. We determine *ex-ante* what the downside could be. That's what we mean by "minimizing surprises".

This is not the same as a philosophy of minimizing risks. The Dragonfly Approach is to decide how much risk you are comfortable taking. Your comfort level with the risks is linked to your desired goals — it affects your goals, while your goals in turn affect your comfort level. We do not endorse an "automatic" preference for reducing risks.

Recap: Deciding Your Risk Appetite

We believe the CEO should have the prerogative to decide the firm's risk appetite — whether to be more "aggressive" or more "conservative". Risk quantification allows you to be clear and specific about how much risk you will be taking relative to your capabilities and capacity. The Dragonfly Risk Appetite Framework laid out in this chapter provides the methodology and the tools to help CEOs and Boards make this crucial decision.

Risk Insights from Chapter 6

Deciding Your Risk Appetite

1. The 3 most important risk issues a CEO and the Board have to make are:

   a. What is the firm's risk appetite?
   b. Does it have the capacity to take that level and mix of risks?
   c. Does it have the capabilities adequate for its risk appetite?

2. Risk appetite is the level and mix of risks you decide to take.

3. Your firm has a specific risk appetite whether you know it or not, and whether you quantify your risks or not.

4. Few organizations are able to make the risk appetite decision confidently. Many are not yet able to quantify all their risks.

5. The Dragonfly Risk Appetite Framework uses 3 quantitative assessments to:

   a. Determine your current (or default) risk appetite;
   b. Determine your target risk appetite (implied by your strategy, plans and budgets); and
   c. Identify your risk appetite constraints.

6. This should be followed by either:

   a. A top-down approach to figure out what the maximum affordable risk appetite is; or
   b. A bottom-up approach to figure out what the required risk appetite is to support the aggregate of all the operating units' budgets.

7. We then iterate between the risk appetite implied by top-down and bottom-up approaches (using the current risk appetite as the baseline), to determine what your risk appetite should be going forward.

8. The risk appetite is the CEO's judgment call – there is no "right answer". Dragonfly believes the decision-making should involve both "science" and "art".

9. "Science" – The Dragonfly Risk Dashboard:

   a. Provides the CEO with comprehensive quantitative information; and
   b. Supports a rigorous process for evaluating the risk underlying the firm's strategy, budgets and resource allocation decisions, which all have risk appetite implications.

10. "Art" – Deciding your risk appetite involves judgment, not just data -- the ambitions for the firm, and what you feel your team and stakeholders are comfortable taking on.

11. Dragonfly believes a philosophy of minimizing *surprises* is more effective than one of minimizing *risks*:

    a. Minimizing surprises means identifying and quantifying in advance:
       - The bets or risk drivers; and
       - The downside impact.
    b. Minimizing surprises is not a pessimistic orientation; it does not suggest we cannot end up with an upside.
    c. Minimizing risks, on the other hand, is a preference for avoiding and reducing risks. It supports the extensive use of controls.

CHAPTER 7

7

WHAT'S YOUR RISK MANAGEMENT PHILOSOPHY?

CEOs know that stakeholders, especially investors, rating agencies and regulators, want to know their firms' risk appetite. Whether the disclosure is adequate or not, stakeholders will form their own impression of the firm. A proactive CEO would want to influence stakeholders' perceptions of the firm's risk profile. In addition to their risk appetite, some CEOs may want to articulate their risk management philosophy.

What constitutes a risk management philosophy? Over our years as risk management practitioners and advisors, we have distilled a set of tenets that we have tested across a diverse range of industries and sectors. We believe you will find this useful as you articulate your own risk management philosophy.

The Dragonfly Risk Management Philosophy is organized into 4 tenets:

1. Purpose and benefits of risk management
2. What risk management is not
3. Common language of risk
4. Deliverables of risk management

1. Purpose and Benefits of Risk Management

The purpose and benefits of risk management are laid out in Exhibit 7.1 and described in some detail in this section.

Exhibit 7.1: Decide What You Want Risk Management to Do

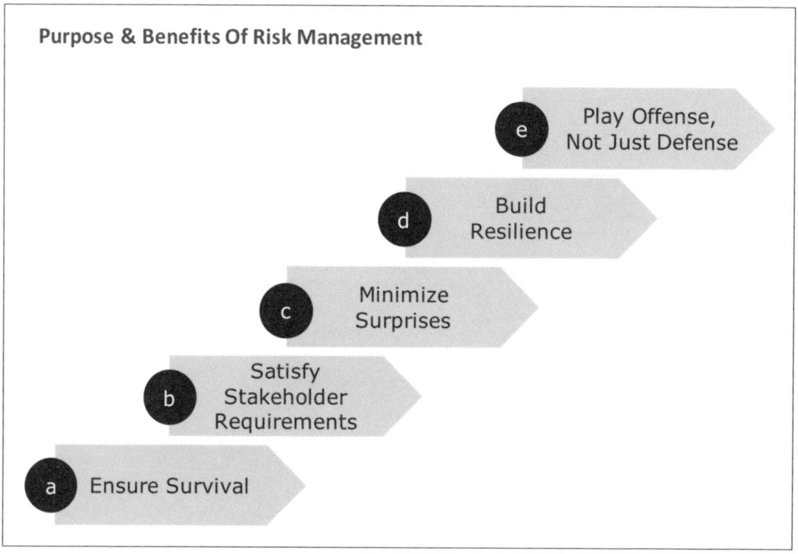

Purpose & Benefits Of Risk Management

e Play Offense, Not Just Defense
d Build Resilience
c Minimize Surprises
b Satisfy Stakeholder Requirements
a Ensure Survival

a. Ensure Survival

At a minimum, every firm needs risk management to ensure that it can survive most sources of risk and severity of shocks. It means that the firm must have the ability to quantify the potential volatility and downside in its cash flow, earnings and balance sheet. It needs to ensure that its capital base and access to liquidity, funding and additional capital are adequate for that potential volatility and downside.

b. Satisfy Stakeholder Requirements

All banks and some non-bank financial businesses are subject to regulations and capital requirements. Many firms are also rated for credit quality by bond rating agencies. Any firm with multiple investors face significant risk scrutiny. This is all the more so when the firm requires significant credit lines from suppliers. At this next level, the purpose of risk management is to assure regulators, rating agencies and other stakeholders that there is adequate risk management at the firm.

c. Minimize Surprises

The next higher purpose is to minimize surprises. It means that we seek to be mindful of the risks as we make our decisions. This is consistent with the principle that risk is neither good nor bad, per se. But risks taken or not taken should be a result of deliberate choices.

We do not seek to minimize risk, or to minimize losses. Instead we aim to know, *ex ante*, how bad the outcomes could be from the risks we take.

We want to know who took those risks and why? What decisions did they take? Which business lines took what risks? What bets on what risk drivers were made? We need to know how much of our risk is due to the size of our exposures, from the sensitivity of the business model/deal structure, and from the potential size of shock.

This tenet is discussed in the last section of Chapter 6.

d. Build Resilience

We believe CEOs should aim to build resilience in their firms.

A firm might suffer setbacks, high volatility or serious downside. Market conditions may be adverse. It might even be a "perfect storm" or a global systemic crisis. A resilient firm is one that does not have to cut its positions summarily, "batten down its hatches", or withdraw from the market to wait out a crisis.

A resilient firm knows where it stands and is not "shell shocked". It looks for and quickly assesses where there might be unusual opportunities. When there are major shocks in the market, there are usually some distressed assets that you can buy at substantially below market value. But these are fleeting opportunities.

66 The Dragonfly Approach enables CEOs to use risk management to play offense -- and compete better. 99

A CEO can only take advantage of such "bargains" if he can quickly assess both the opportunity and his firm's capacity to act. He also needs to be able to mobilize his organization and meet corporate governance requirements faster than normal.

Even if such unusual opportunities are not present, a firm led by a CEO who can "bounce back" from adverse conditions quickly will outperform its rivals. Hence, resilience is a powerful purpose and competitive reason for building risk management.

e. Play Offense, Not Just Defense

Many CEOs see risk management as a necessary but defensive tool. The Dragonfly Approach to risk management is designed to go beyond the defensive role – to enable a CEO to play offense, by using risk data and analytics to find better ways to compete.

Most well-run firms already have strong processes to continually develop better and/or cheaper products for their customers. However, our experience shows that very few firms have used risk management capabilities to improve their products. The risk characteristics or preferences of their customers are a largely untapped area. Customers are often unprepared or unwilling to take risk and would like the sellers to absorb the price or supply risk. Unfortunately, many seller firms instinctively shy away from taking such risks.

Our emphasis on quantification helps clients understand risk better. The data and insights from risk quantification can be used to develop or structure better products for customers. The risk analytics and tools can be used to help price and manage risks better. It helps clients compete better. This is what we mean by playing offense, and not just defense.

2. What Risk Management Is Not

As part of articulating your philosophy, we believe it is just as important for CEOs to understand what risk management *is not*.

There are four common objectives that involve risk, which we believe should *not* be confused with the enterprise-wide risk management that is the focus of this book:

a. Hedging
b. Forecasting
c. Buy/Sell model
d. Preventing losses

a. <u>Hedging</u>
Many confuse hedging with risk management. It is a tool of risk management, but it should not be the *goal* of risk management, per se.

Hedging is the decision to change the amount of a risk taken. For example, an airline uses 100,000 gallons of jet fuel for a particular route per month. It might feel that the risk of fuel prices rising over the next 12 months is too high.

This could be because its revenues are to a large degree fixed, because, e.g. it has presold many of the seats. To protect its margins, it could reduce the risk of fuel price rising by hedging, i.e. reducing its vulnerability to the impact of an oil price rise on the 100,000 gallons used per month.

At first glance, this might seem a "no-brainer"; isn't risk reduction always a good thing? Upon further evaluation, however, we will realize that while hedging changes our risk profile, it does not necessarily eliminate all risk. In the example, our hypothetical airline would have reduced its risk to fuel price rising, say, by locking in the price of the 100,000 gallons required. But what if the fuel price falls instead of rising?

If fuel prices fell by, say 20%, this airline would have forgone a margin improvement on the presold seats. The cost per seat would be lower if it had not hedged its fuel price risk. If the airline still has unsold seats, its ability to offer reduced prices on those seats is impacted by the higher, locked-in fuel cost from its hedging. Therefore, its ability to compete aggressively to sell the remaining seats is also adversely affected. So in our example, while hedging reduces the risk of rising fuel price and alters the firm's risk profile, it now exposes the firm to the risk of falling fuel prices.

Hedging is therefore only a *tool* of risk management. It is not, in and of itself, the *purpose* of risk management. The CEO has to decide, on a case-by-case basis, whether or not to hedge a risk position.

b. Forecasting

In forecasting, you make your best guess at the future level of a particular parameter. A more sophisticated forecast would include the expected margin of error.

There is a lot of similarity between forecasting and risk management. But forecasting is *not* risk management. In risk, we need to predict the full set of possible outcomes regardless of probability. In forecasting, we are usually trying to make the best guess of the *most likely single* outcome.

In risk, we are more concerned with not omitting the extreme downsides and less concerned about precision. In forecasting, however, we are less concerned about the extreme downside, as that would be a highly unlikely event.

Forecasting is a critical function in its own right and a useful tool for risk management. But it is not a purpose or benefit of risk management.

> " Stakeholders, especially investors, rating agencies and regulators want to know their firms' risk appetites. Whether the disclosure is adequate or not, stakeholders will form their own impression of the firm. "

Exhibit 7.2: What Risk Management Is Not

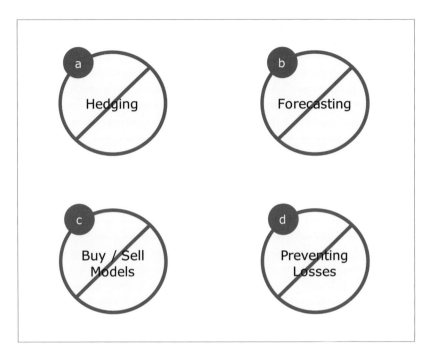

c. Buy/Sell Models

Some executives mistakenly expect risk management models to be able to tell a CEO when to buy or sell an asset, or take or shed risks. Such models require much of the same data, analysis and know-how that a good risk manager provides.

However, prescribing buy/sell decisions is not the objective of risk management models. For risk management, we do not restrict ourselves to the most likely future values. We want to know the *full range* of possible values with their respective probabilities, especially on the downside.

To make a buy/sell decision, it is necessary to predict the most likely future outcome or value. So even if the model itself is the same, the choice of inputs to run the model is very different for buy/sell decisions, compared to risk decisions.

We use risk models to determine what the potential downside could be, how much volatility we need to be able to handle, and how much capital is required. We compare this with our capacity to handle the potential volatility and downside, and determine if we can price adequately for the risks we would need to take. Together with the understanding of what our customers' needs and risk preferences are, we decide whether to take the risk, i.e. we decide our risk appetite. Therefore, risk management is more multifaceted than buy/sell modeling.

d. Preventing Losses

CEOs get this piece of erroneous advice from time to time – that a risk management system will help prevent losses. Proponents of the Control Self Assessment approach (see Chapter 8) often make this mistake.

Preventing losses as an approach leads to minimizing risks taken, increasing controls, finding ways to pass the risk to the customer and suppliers. This stifles the business lines and reduces the attractiveness of the firm's offerings to its customers.

Hence, Dragonfly advises CEOs that the goal of risk management should not be to minimize losses. Instead, as discussed earlier, it should be to minimize *surprises*.

The critical factor is in the intent — focus on deciding what amount and mix of risk the firm wants to take. This is in order to actively manage the business to try to avoid the downside, while aiming to achieve an outcome that is from the more favorable parts of the distribution of possible outcomes.

Taking and managing the risks that come with specific business decisions or transactions is an integral part of the value proposition to a customer. It can be as valuable to the client as the technology or physical attributes of what we are selling. Hence, minimizing risks merely to prevent losses cannot be consistent with an attractive and competitive strategy.

3. Common Language of Risk

A core component of Dragonfly's Risk Management Philosophy is that the firm must use a common language for risk, just as accounting is a common language for performance measurement, and finance is a universal language for communicating about funding and investment.

When everyone in a firm uses a common language for risk management, there can be consistent understanding of the facts, assumptions, tradeoffs and the judgment calls to be made. Only then can discussions be truly constructive.

We have seen numerous well-meaning executives mired in dysfunctional debates because they are unaware that there is inconsistency in definitions and/or calibrations. For example, I might view a particular deal structure as "high risk" whereas you feel it is "modest risk". We could *both* be correct. It is just that we are looking at different levels of outcomes, both of which are possible. Or it could be because we have different risk appetites. Part of a common language is the standardization of how risks are quantified. Without a common language, our debate could be interminable. Worse, our disagreements can start to become confrontational, leading to dysfunction.

The key ingredients of a common language for risk management are:

a. All Risks – we must include all sources of risks affecting the firm.

b. Quantified – all risks must be quantified. The appropriate risk metrics must be selected for the firm's goals. The impact on the goals from all sources of risks must be measured.

c. Risk-Return Mindset – the approach to reviewing, communicating and deciding on risk should focus on this question: "What are the possible returns I can earn for the risks I am taking?"

66 A resilient firm is one that does not have to cut its positions summarily, 'batten down its hatches' or withdraw from the market to wait out a crisis. 99

Exhibit 7.3: Common Language of Risk

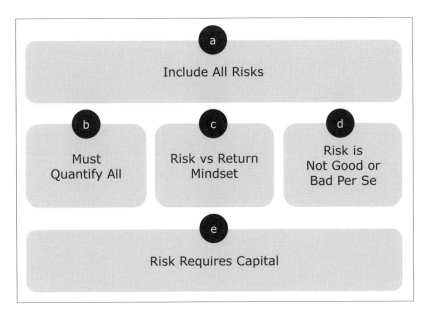

d. Risk is Neither Good nor Bad – Dragonfly is "agnostic" about the level of risks, per se. By itself, a risk is neither good nor bad. The justification for taking a level of risk comes from the possible returns that taking the risk could provide. It is a "good" risk if the potential returns adequately justify the cost of the risk taken. This can be measured by the potential return on the risk capital required.

e. Risk Requires Capital -- The amount of capital a firm requires depends on the amount of risk it is taking. Each firm needs to set the degree of "protection", or cushion against insolvency that it requires. These are also called the risk capital parameters. Risk capital is the common metric for comparing different activities and different sources of risk. Capital is also typically the most important scarce resource for a firm.

Any firm that uses the 5 components we described above will be able to build a common risk language.

4. Deliverables of Risk Management

Many CEOs think of risk management as a set of policies, procedures and reports for complying with regulatory and capital requirements. They have nagging doubts about the buy-in within their firm and ultimately, the effectiveness and benefits of the costly and controversial efforts required.

The Dragonfly Risk Management Philosophy contends that if CEOs focus on the appropriate deliverables, the risk management process will be effective and produce real benefits. This is true whether it is a "first generation" program or an advanced version of risk management. (See Exhibit 7.4 next page)

66 When everyone in a firm uses a common language for risk management, there can be consistent understanding of the facts, assumptions, tradeoffs and the judgment calls to be made. Only then can discussions be truly constructive. 99

Exhibit 7.4: The Dragonfly Risk Philosophy Aims to Provide Data,
Dialogue & Decisions for CEOs to Manage Uncertainty

The deliverables we aim for are the same — regardless of the
sophistication or scale of the firm's risk management:

a. Data - timely, comprehensive data on exposures to all
   causes of risk, organized by risk driver and responsibility
   center.

b. Dialogue - management debate should include the
   risks involved in a decision. Our approach is to integrate
   risk data and analytics into the firm's existing decision-
   making process, including budgeting, strategy and
   investment processes.

c. Decisions - when risk is part of the management decision-
   making process, we know the function is a success. Most
   top management decisions involve making judgment
   calls about future conditions under uncertainty.

Recap: What's Your Risk Management Philosophy?

In addition to deciding on the firm's risk appetite (as discussed in Chapter 6), a CEO should be prepared to lay out his overall risk management philosophy.

This chapter discusses The Dragonfly Risk Management Philosophy, which is organized around four principles:

1. Consciousness of the purpose and benefits of risk management.
2. Knowing what risk management is *not*.
3. Building a common language of risk management.
4. Focusing on the deliverables of risk management — Data, Dialogue and Decisions.

> "If CEOs focus on data, dialogue and decisions, the risk management process will be effective and produce clear benefits."

Risk Insights from Chapter 7

What's Your Risk Management Philosophy?

CEOs should articulate their risk management philosophy to their stakeholders.

The Dragonfly Risk Management Philosophy is organized around 4 principles:

1. Consciousness of the purpose and benefits of risk management:

    a. Ensuring survival of the firm
    b. Satisfying stakeholder requirements
    c. Minimizing surprises
    d. Building resilience
    e. Playing offense, not just defense

2. Knowing what risk management is *not*. The following are not the purpose of risk management per se:

    a. Hedging
    b. Forecasting
    c. Buy/Sell model
    d. Preventing losses

3. Building a common language of risk management with the following elements:

   a. Including all sources of risk
   b. Acceptance that all risks must be quantified, with risk metrics linked to firm's goals
   c. A Risk-Return mindset where everyone asks what the possible returns are for the risks being taken
   d. Quantification of the capital required for the risk appetite chosen

4. Focus on the deliverables of risk management:

   a. Data – timely, comprehensive and complete data, segmented by risk driver and responsibility
   b. Dialogue – all management dialogue should include the evaluation of risk implications
   c. Decisions – risk data and analytics must be useful, and used in management decisions

CHAPTER 8

8

WHY MANY COMMON RISK MANAGEMENT PRACTICES ARE FLAWED

Control Self Assessment (CSA) is a common risk management approach, due to its simplicity and its purported ease in getting organisational buy-in. CSA was developed from the laudable attempts by regulators and the auditing profession to deal with cases involving large and sensational failures in internal controls, corporate and risk governance, such as Enron (2001), WorldCom (2002) and Parmalat (2003).

The CSA approach uses structured interviews covering the entire organization. Representatives from each organizational unit identify and assess the risks and controls of activities in their respective units – hence the "self-assessment" in the name.

The risk metric used is based on a scoring method: a composite of the likelihood (L) of each possible risk incident, on a scale of (typically) 1 to 5, and the severity of impact (I) of the risk, also on a scale of 1 to 5. The risk score is LxI – minimum of 1 (as in 1x1) to a maximum of 25 (5x5). (See Exhibit 8.1).

Exhibit 8.1: Control Self Assessment – Risk Scoring Methodology

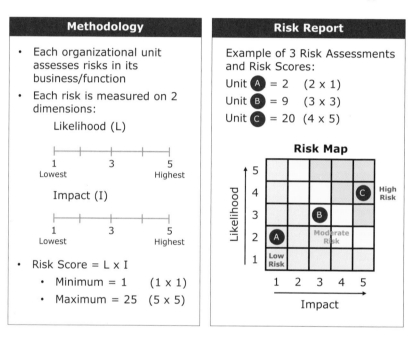

The resulting risk scores for each potential risk identified, for all the organizational units, are consolidated into a "risk register". The top risks (typically the top 10) are then displayed in a "traffic lights" report or risk map. This is typically shown in a 5x5 grid. The likelihood is shown on the vertical axis and the impact on the horizontal axis. The top risks are typically sorted into 3 categories for management attention: high (>=15 risk score); moderate (risk score of 8 to 12); low (risk score of 1 to 6). This is often represented as red, yellow and green respectively, hence the analogy to "traffic lights".

Erroneous Views of CSA, ERM & VaR

The CSA approach is sometimes called Enterprise Risk Management (ERM). However, to do so is inaccurate and improper because:

- There are other approaches to ERM that do *not* use CSA. The Dragonfly Approach discussed in this book is an example.
- As CSA is not a proper quantitative methodology, many users *erroneously* assume that ERM therefore cannot be quantitative. The Dragonfly Approach shows that all the risks in an enterprise *can* be quantified.

This mistake leads to **another** erroneous view – that Value at Risk (VaR) is quantitative management, whereas ERM is not. Although VaR is a quantitative tool, it is *not* the only such tool. Neither is VaR a risk metric that is suitable to assess *all* the risks that exist in an organization.

Flaws in CSA Methodology

In this chapter, we wish to **warn CEOs of the flaws in the CSA concept and methodology**:

1. Simplistic Risk Definition
2. Misleading Measurements / Improper Quantification
3. Risk Reports Limited in Usefulness
4. Illusory Ease of Buy-in
5. Gives False Sense of Assurance

While not wholly discredited, the flaws of CSA will not only limit the effectiveness of risk management, they may even blindside CEOs. The final section of this chapter will discuss options for CEOs whose firms are using a CSA framework.

1. Simplistic Risk Definition

In CSA, risk is defined and measured as the risk score: likelihood x impact of a risk outcome. The risk score is assessed by a risk owner or participant in the CSA process.

Exhibit 8.2 below shows the risk distribution of production yields in a factory. For example, the risk owner might assess the risk score as 8, (see X: 2x4). He sees the risk as the production yield falling to 75%, instead of the targeted 85%.

Exhibit 8.2: The Commonly Used Risk Metric – Risk Score – Is Simplistic

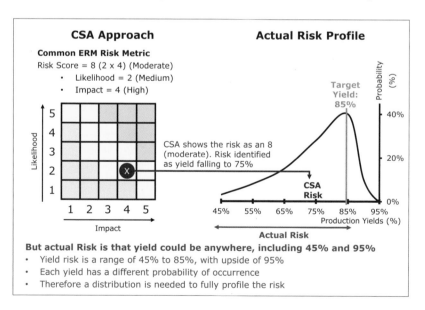

At first blush, the simplicity and user-friendliness of The CSA grid is attractive. It is, however, deceptive. If one looks at the risk distribution, one will see that the risk – the potential downside in production yield – could be 75%, 65% or worse, all the way down to 45%. The risk is not only the case of the yield falling to 75% (or X in Exhibit 8.2, previous page).

But CSA does *not* use risk distributions. Risk is not defined the way Dragonfly does in Chapter 1, i.e. the chance that one may not attain one's goals, which in this case is the target yield of 85%. With CSA, the risk owner is asked only for a simple risk score. He will be picking only one specific point from the underlying risk distribution. In our illustration earlier, he would have picked A or B but not both. He would certainly not be asked to depict the entire risk distribution.

The CSA approach also gives the false impression that risk has been quantified just because the risk score is numeric. However, as we can see from Exhibit 7.2, the appropriate risk metric here should be the production yield (or the shortfall in production yield). It is not a *score* of between 1 and 25. Just because a CSA risk score is numeric doesn't make it an appropriate risk quantification metric.

Proponents of CSA argue that risk scoring is a way of standardizing risk measurement so that different risk types can be compared using the same metric. However, CSA's approach to standardization and comparability is still too simplistic. The next section will discuss The Dragonfly Approach to Risk Quantification and how it ensures robust standardization and comparability.

The Dragonfly Approach to Risk Quantification

Instead of the CSA methodology of risk scoring, Dragonfly uses two robust methodologies for standardization and comparability:

    a. Using goal(s)/target(s) to define the risk metric.

    b. Standardizing the confidence level at which to measure the downside risk.

a. <u>Appropriate Risk Metric</u>

In Exhibit 8.3 below, we evaluate two different risks — production yield downside and pricing shortfalls.

Exhibit 8.3: CSA Risk Score May Not Be the Appropriate Risk Metric

Example 1	Example 2
CSA Approach Risk of **75%** Yield: **Target Yield: 85%** • (L = 2) x (I = 4) • Risk Score = 8 	**CSA Approach** Risk of **$0.90** price **Target Price: $1.10** • (L = 2) x (I = 5) • Risk Score = 10 
Dragonfly Risk Metric: Earnings • Risk is quantified as 20 percentage points in yield drop from the 85% target -- a 24% fall • Converted into earnings downside	**Dragonfly Risk Metric: Earnings** • Risk is quantified as 20 cents drop in price from the $1.10 target -- an 18% fall • Converted into earnings downside

CSA uses risk scores as the risk metric. In this example, production yield risk (left chart) is an 8. Price risk (right chart) is a 10.

The Dragonfly Approach, however uses earnings as the risk metric in this example. Both risk drivers in this example -- production yield shortfalls and price downsides -- cause downside in earnings. (See Chapter 1 for a discussion on how to select risk metrics).

In practice, even across different industries, there are only a handful of risk metrics that CEOs need to focus on, regardless of the number of organizational units or risk drivers.

The Dragonfly Approach does *not* use risk scoring. Instead, we select the risk metric that best apply to the goal being assessed.

With the CSA approach, although the risk scores are different (8 for yield risk versus 10 for price risk) it is not clear what the 2-point difference actually means. This is an example of why CSA is simplistic and risk scores do *not* work well as risk metrics.

b. <u>Standardizing Confidence Level</u>
Dragonfly also recommends that CEOs decide on a specific confidence level of risk as a standardized parameter to measure all risks. This is necessary because risk is always a probability distribution of possible outcomes, not a single outcome.

For example, what is the 99th percentile worst-case downside, for any goal, due to any risk driver?

You will recognize this as the same concept used in Value at Risk (VaR) – the 99th percentile downside in valuation. (*Please see Chapter 4 for a full discussion of risk quantification*).

The CSA approach, however, does not standardize the confidence level at which to measure the downside. In fact, it does not expect the risk assessor to determine the underlying risk distribution. Instead it gives the assessor the discretion to pick a specific level of risk (impact) and its associated likelihood.

Even if the assessor recognizes that there is an underlying distribution of possible outcomes, he has total discretion as to which specific downside outcome he perceives as "the" risk. Hence, 3 different assessors may pick 3 different points from the same risk distribution, and the result will be 3 different risk scores. There is no standardization of the confidence level of the underlying distribution.

2. Misleading Measurements (or Improper Quantifications)

The CSA approach has serious flaws in how it measures risk:

   a. It does not distinguish between likely and unexpected downsides.
   b. Risk scores tend to understate severe downside levels.
   c. Extreme downside risk tends to be omitted altogether due to the nature of the assessment process.

> " The CSA approach is sometimes called Enterprise Risk Management. However, to do so is inaccurate and improper. "

a. <u>Failure to Distinguish Likely and Unexpected Downsides</u>
The downside risks of an activity can be segmented into two types – "likely" case and "extreme" case.

For illustration, let's define a "likely" case as an event with a 33% probability of occurrence, and an extreme case as an event with a 1% probability of occurrence. We illustrate this in Exhibit 8.4, which shows the distribution of possible accident rates for a large construction project.

Exhibit 8.4: Construction Worksite Accident Rate

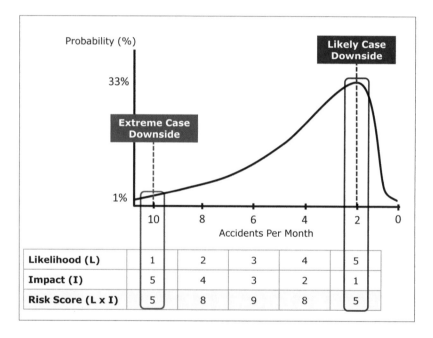

The CSA approach does not distinguish between these two very different probabilities of downside.

A "likely" case accident rate would have an L of 5 and an I of 1 – giving it a risk score of 5. Meanwhile, for the "extreme" case accident rate, it would be assessed with an L of 1 and an I of 5. This also results in a CSA risk score of 5.

Both types of downside – the "likely" and the "extreme" – are important to measure and evaluate. But since the CSA approach does not distinguish between the two, it would be unlikely that *both* will be assessed. Further, we would never really know *which* one is picked as we would see the *same* risk score of 5.

The distinction is important as the risk management implications of "likely" and "extreme" events are strikingly different.

In this example the "likely" case event has a relatively modest impact – 2 accidents a month, medical expenses, plus physical rehabilitation costs. However, since it is much more likely to happen, safety control processes, training and monitoring programs are all feasible and should be put in place. "Likely" events are also more predictable, and there are typically enough options for managing this type of risk.

In the same example, there is only a 1% chance that the project suffers from 10 or more accidents per month. While "extreme" case events are very low probability, they can have highly severe direct costs, and may also have legal, reputational and regulatory ramifications. Therefore, in addition to the typical safety and control processes, contingency plans, crisis management and communication protocols, it may be necessary to buy insurance coverage. These additional risk management options are often more onerous and require more evaluation and structuring.

In practice, it is not only crucial to distinguish between "likely" and "extreme" case events, but also to ensure that the risk quantification methodology specifies which probability of downside risk to measure, and further, to ensure that it is done consistently across-the-board.

As we have shown, the CSA approach is not designed to do that; it uses far too simplistic a definition of risk and it does not quantify risks properly. Hence, it fails to distinguish the "likely" from the "extreme" downsides.

b. <u>CSA Tends to Understate Severe Downside Risks</u>
Another serious flaw of the CSA methodology is that severe downside risks are systematically understated. Typically, severe downside risks are very low probability events – for example, extreme weather-related property loss. Such a risk would carry a risk score of 5 (1x5), with the lowest likelihood score of 1 and the highest impact score of 5. A risk score of 5 would be shown as a "yellow" or moderate risk in the CSA risk map or "traffic lights" matrix. Such a low risk score would not get management attention.

This is very misleading. If the incident occurs, the downside is severe and management should be aware of this contingency. However, with the way CSA works, severe downside risks are unlikely to score higher than a 5 on a scale of 1 to 25, as the low probability of extreme downside risks would mean likelihood (L) is scored as a 1.

c. Extreme Downside Risks May Be Omitted Altogether Due to the Nature of the Assessment Process
Even worse, the CSA approach tends to omit many extreme downside events, since it does not lay out the full distribution of outcomes. Further, the CSA interview approach makes it difficult to ensure uniform and consistent calibration of risks across participants.

When we think about risk, most of us tend to be biased towards "likely" downside events. Therefore, the results of CSA interviews will tend to omit risks that are low probability but have severe potential downside.

We gain most of our perspectives from our day-to-day experiences. Therefore, we tend to see risk as the downside we have experienced or dealt with most often. Also, most of us value optimism and generally prefer to show a more positive picture to ourselves and to senior management. This is reinforced by the typical mandates given to the businesses; for investment decisions, senior management usually ask the business lines about "likely" outcomes, rather than about "extreme" outcomes.

 " Risk is always a probability distribution of possible outcomes, not a single outcome. "

For example, in Exhibit 8.5 below, most CSA users would assess the risk of a terrorist attack as the possibility of a medium impact incident. They would miss the very low probability case of a catastrophic attack (right tail of distribution).

Exhibit 8.5: Risk Distribution of Terrorist Attacks

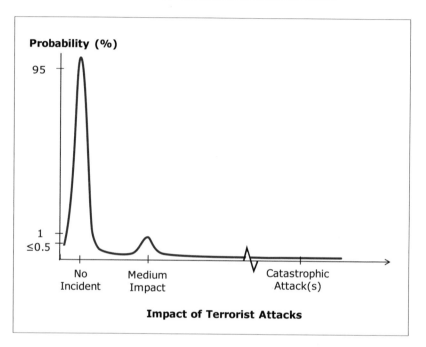

3. CSA Risk Reports Are Limited in Usefulness

The CSA "Traffic Lights" approach appears attractive because of its simplicity, and because it helps CEOs focus on the "Top Risks".

However, it is of limited usefulness as:

- There are blind spots in the report due to structural weaknesses in the CSA approach. As discussed earlier, risk scores may understate risks, while extreme risks may be omitted altogether.
- An organization may be hit materially by a risk that does not make the list of "Top Risks". For example, a risk ranked 22nd on the list could occur. It may be a large loss, but management would not have been forewarned as it did not make the top 10 list.

- Risk scores are not well linked to business objectives. Examples include: difficulty in making sense of a risk score when making a pricing decision; translating a risk score to the cost of managing the risk or to the capital required for the risk taken. Hence, the CSA approach is limited in providing insights or practical options for decision-making.

4. Illusory Ease of Buy-In

The principal reason for the popularity of CSA is the supposed ease of buy-in by the organization for risk management. It appears to be a simple approach that can be easily and quickly implemented across an organization. Also, because the risk owners themselves do the assessments, it seems there would be buy-in to both the assessment process and the risk data generated. Further, it is plausible to assume that the risk data is more credible because the risk owners should be the experts in their respective areas and activities.

Unfortunately, CSA's promise of buy-in is illusory. Any acceptance is at best temporary. This is due to inherent flaws in the CSA approach:

- CSA's promise of simplicity is undermined by its simplistic methodology. This becomes apparent from a deeper and more thoughtful look at the approach, when flaws such as inappropriate risk definition and misleading measurements show up upon implementation.

- The self-assessment process is tedious and time consuming. In practice, participants often resort to "copy and paste" or a cursory update in the next annual cycle of self-assessment.

- As discussed earlier, the CSA approach produces little demonstrable benefits aside from compliance with corporate governance guidelines. Without such benefits, any buy-in obtained is unsustainable. Business lines may simply "check the boxes" to show compliance with the process. This does *not* produce effective risk management.

- The emphasis on controls and risk mitigation underpinning the CSA methodology inhibits buy-in. Users find the emphasis on controls stifling. To stay competitive, most business lines have to dynamically evaluate and decide what risks to take, how to price them, and how to manage them. The CSA approach, however, tends to overemphasize the mitigation of risks and eventually erodes actual buy-in.

5. Gives a False Sense of Assurance

The CSA approach may appear to provide comprehensive risk data, adequate controls and substantial risk mitigation. However, the CEO still cannot "sleep well at night" because:

a. Controls and mitigation, although useful, are inadequate for effective risk management;
b. Risks may be higher than the CSA reports show; and
c. A risk type may be transformed into a different risk rather than effectively mitigated or truly reduced.

a. <u>An Overemphasis on Controls and Risk Mitigation</u>

The CSA approach "treats" the risks identified by finding ways to reduce their likelihood and/or impact, thereby reducing the number of risks shown as "Reds" and "Yellows" in the firm's portfolio. This tends to regard all risks as undesirable – to be controlled, mitigated and reduced. As a result, whether intentional or not, CSA's processes take on an audit or "risk police" tone. Even the name "Control Self Assessment" reinforces this perspective.

While controls and risk mitigation are important tools, they should not be overemphasized. A better approach is to evaluate the risk-return profile (range of upside and downside) of different business choices to consider:

- What level and mix of risks to take? What is the firm's risk appetite in different environments?
- Which risks to take? To what extent are we qualified to take them? What risks are we paid adequately to take?

- How does risk impact pricing, product structuring, and the design/configuration of operational processes?

Unfortunately, the Control Self Assessment approach overemphasizes controls and mitigation instead of providing data and analysis to support these critical business decisions.

b. <u>A Mistaken Conclusion That the Firm's Risks Are Lower</u>
With CSA, users may conclude – incorrectly – that a firm is not taking substantial risks. Even for well-run firms, it can be misleading since the CSA methodology is unlikely to produce many risks in the "red", or even "yellow" categories.

This is because management of well-run firms would have dealt with most of the high-likelihood events. If the risk is highly likely to occur, it is also usually somewhat predictable, and the causal drivers more observable. As a result, the CSA approach would not show much risk.

At the same time, the CSA approach systematically understates the lower likelihood risks by assigning them low risk scores. As we have seen earlier:

- Many severe downside events tend to have low likelihood (and hence low CSA risk scores, shown as "yellows") when in fact the risk can be devastating. For example, CSA would indicate the risk of a terrorist attack as "yellow", when in fact, it is a high downside impact event.

- "Extreme" case risks may be systematically ignored and omitted. The large downside level may not be captured since CSA does not evaluate or depict the full distribution of possible outcomes. For example, the risk of an investment project may be depicted as a sub-par IRR, which would be a "yellow". The fact that there is a small chance that the project could suffer a loss of principal – a more severe risk – may be omitted as the assessor picked the more likely downside of a sub-par IRR.

c. A False Sense of Comfort in Mitigation

The emphasis on risk mitigation in CSA, as well as the very name of the process itself ("Control Self Assessment"), lulls management into a false sense of comfort. It suggests that risks once identified, can be mitigated through hedging and control processes. The resulting environment is assumed to be well-controlled, implying there is little residual risk.

However, having strong controls does not necessarily mean taking low risk. Further, not all risk mitigation attempts are sustainable. Worse, some do not actually reduce the overall risk for the user. Instead, the risk is often transformed from one risk type to another.

For example, a firm might manage its vendor risk by setting tough legal policies, with terms and conditions such as penalties for non-performance. We had a client who took pride in "bullet-proofing" their contracts and in so doing, felt they had mitigated their risks.

If a major vendor of this client fails to perform and the incident leads to serious disruptions of service to its customers, our client would then claim financial compensation from its vendor. However, if the vendor is unable to pay up fully, the mitigation of performance risk by "bullet-proofing" the contracts is a failure. The legal risk is now transformed into credit risk. Further, the disruption of service would create reputational risk for the client.

What started out as vendor risk, which was to have been mitigated by the strong contract, became transformed into credit and reputational risk downsides.

Recap: Why Many Common Risk Management Practices Are Flawed

We have laid out the 5 serious flaws in the popular CSA methodology. Although firms might benefit from the wider risk awareness and assessment of controls that the CSA process enables, its limitations must not be ignored. What does this mean for CEOs, investors and regulators?

66 We believe that CEOs, investors and regulators need to be aware of the serious limitations of the CSA approach and work urgently on improving their risk quantification and management capabilities. 99

Exhibit 8.6: Be Aware That Some Common Risk Practices Are Flawed

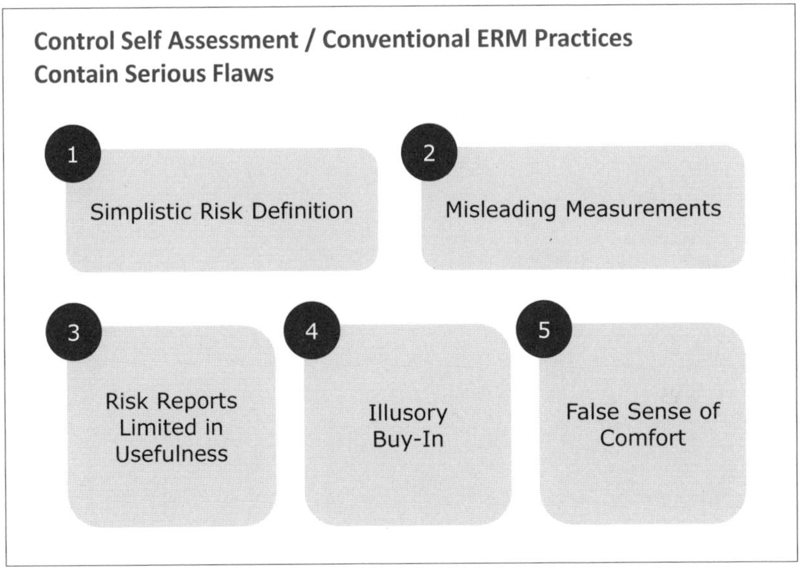

Control Self Assessment / Conventional ERM Practices Contain Serious Flaws

1 Simplistic Risk Definition

2 Misleading Measurements

3 Risk Reports Limited in Usefulness

4 Illusory Buy-In

5 False Sense of Comfort

The true test of a good risk management process is in the kind of decisions it can help us make, the kind of behaviours it encourages or discourages, and the extent to which it aligns risk-taking with the objectives and capabilities of the firm. Effective risk management prepares decision makers to be more resilient in turbulent conditions. In addition, by helping us take smarter risks, we are more likely to capture the upside potential and maximize returns.

Unfortunately, CSA does not provide the necessary tools to do this due to its flawed methodology and weakness in quantification.

We believe that CEOs, investors and regulators need to be aware of the serious limitations of the CSA approach and work urgently on improving their risk quantification and management capabilities.

Risk Insights from Chapter 8

Why Many Common Risk Management Practices Are Flawed

1. Control Self Assessment (CSA) is a very common risk management approach due to its simplicity and the promise of ease in getting organizational buy-in.

2. CSA uses structured interviews with representatives from each organizational unit to perform "self assessment" in identifying risk.

3. The risk metric used is a compound score of:

    a. The likelihood of each risk incident on a scale of 1 to 5 (5 being highest); and

    b. The impact of the risk, on a scale of 1 to 5 (5 being the most severe impact).

    Risk scores therefore range from 1 to 25 (1x1 to 5x5).

4. The risk scores for every risk identified are consolidated into a "risk register". The top risks are displayed in a "traffic lights" grid – red for high risk, followed by yellow, and green (for low risk).

5. The CSA approach is sometimes erroneously called Enterprise Risk Management (ERM). It is also often erroneously considered to be the qualitative portion of risk management, to complement Value at Risk (VaR) which is thought to cover all the risks that can be quantified in the organization.

6. Unfortunately, despite its popularity and the promise of organizational buy-in, CSA is flawed and therefore limited in effectiveness. Its 5 main flaws are:

   a. Simplistic Risk Definition – The risk score is only a single point in the underlying risk distribution; although it is numeric, it uses a single crude metric for all risks.

   b. Misleading Measurements / Improper Quantification:
      • No distinction between "likely" and "unexpected" downsides;
      • Understatement of severe downside risk due to nature of risk scoring; and
      • Tendency to omit "extreme" downside risk.

   c. Limited Usefulness of Risk Reports – CSA "Traffic Lights" and "Top Risks" are easy to use, but a firm could be hit by a risk that did not make the list. Further, risk scores are not well linked to business objectives or decisions.

   d. Illusory Ease of Buy-In – In practice, there is little actual buy-in because:
      • Users realize that risk measurement in CSA is simplistic;
      • Self assessments are tedious and time-consuming;
      • There are no demonstrable benefits beyond compliance with governance guidelines; and
      • Emphasis on controls stifles the business lines.

e. False Sense of Assurance
   - Controls and mitigation are useful but inadequate for managing risk;
   - Actual risks may be higher than CSA reports show; and
   - Risks may be transformed rather than mitigated.

7. The 5 flaws limit the effectiveness of risk management and may even blindside the CEO.

8. The true test of risk management is in the kinds of decisions and behaviors they encourage in the firm, that allow for smarter risk-taking and organizational resilience in turbulent conditions.

9. CEOs, investors and regulators need to be aware of the limitations of the CSA approach and work on urgently improving risk capabilities, especially in proper quantification.

CHAPTER 9

9

MAKING RISK MANAGEMENT EFFECTIVE IN PRACTICE

As a CEO, you're well aware of the need for risk management, and you have put in place risk specialists and risk management processes. However, we believe that like many of the CEOs we've met, you have doubts about the effectiveness of risk management *in practice*.

Does your risk management adequately help you understand and manage the risks you take? Does it support what the business lines need to do in order to satisfy your customers competitively and also earn an adequate return?

It is not just the effectiveness in your organization that concerns you. Reading the Financial Times and the Wall Street Journal, you will notice that again and again, there have been cases of failures in risk management – not just at financial institutions, but also at companies in different sectors, government agencies and non-profit institutions.

In this chapter, we will share with you what we believe it takes to make risk management effective in practice. Dragonfly has been continually involved in risk management for the last 25+ years – from our pioneering days developing the methodology, as practitioners building and running the global risk management function for a leading investment bank, and in the most recent 20 years, as risk advisors to CEOs in many sectors. In all our work, the ultimate test is the effectiveness of what we develop and recommend.

In this chapter, we will discuss **The Dragonfly Approach for making risk management effective**. It is organized into **7 imperatives**:

1. CEOs must take leadership in risk
2. Expect resistance and do not wait for buy-in
3. Don't depend on committees
4. Use *both* independence *and* partnership
5. Data, dialogue, decisions
6. It is *both* science *and* art
7. Develop a risk culture that fits

1. CEO Leadership in Risk Management

All CEOs know that risks are taken by business lines, as well as by support functions throughout the firm. Unfortunately, not all CEOs appreciate that they "inherit" – and hence own – all the risks taken by everyone, everywhere in the organization.

All CEOs want their business line and functional heads to take ownership of and manage the risks arising from their activities. CEOs also hope that their direct reports embrace the development and application of risk management. In practice, very few are satisfied that this actually happens.

Instead of waiting for this ideal state to materialize, Dragonfly recommends that you, as CEO, demonstrate clear leadership in risk management. We believe you must acknowledge that you own all the risks, enterprise-wide. You need to send a clear signal that evaluating, deciding and managing the risks at the portfolio level is your job. You also need to show that as CEO, managing risk is as important a role as setting strategy, allocating capital and resources, and managing your direct reports. This is one of the 7 imperatives that make risk management effective in practice.

Whose Job is Risk Management?
We do not, however, mean that managing risk is *only* the CEO's job. Dragonfly takes pains to emphasize to clients that risk management is the job of not just the CEO, but *also* the job of business line/functional heads. They directly generate the risk and are therefore best equipped to evaluate why the risk is justified, and how it can be managed cost-effectively. Product structuring and pricing are obvious examples.

Although critical, the efforts of the direct risk owners will not be sufficient. Risks must also be evaluated and managed at the CEO level, i.e. enterprise-wide or at the group portfolio level. For example, each and every one of the business lines might take the appropriate risks at their individual levels and manage them well. But in aggregate, at the enterprise level, it might be too high a risk appetite. It might also create too much concentration in a particular type of risk.

Exhibit 9.1: Whose Job is Risk Management?

Whose Job Is Risk Management?

	Business Line /Functional Dept	vs	CEO
Risk	Direct Source of Risk	←→	"Inherited" from organic units/activities
Level/Scope	At Individual Unit Level / "Own" Risks	←→	Enterprise-wide Level & Mix
Timeframe	Product / Transaction Shorter Term	←→	Reporting Cycle / Longer Term
Probability	Likely / Expected Outcomes	←→	Very Low Probability / Extreme Impact
Focus	Product Structure Pricing Customer	←→	Resource/Capital Allocation Ratings, Investors, Regulators

The CEO needs to consider the longer-term horizon, whereas the direct risk owner has to focus on the shorter term or the period covered by each transaction.

The CEO has to be alert to low probability but extreme shocks, whereas the business line should concentrate on the more likely or expected outcomes.

Finally, firm-wide resource allocation, credit ratings, investor and regulatory implications of risk management are best handled at the CEO level. Because of all the aforementioned critical differences in perspective, the CEO has to lead in risk management, even if the business line and functional heads take full ownership of their respective risks.

Even the Best CRO is Not Enough

Many CEOs believe that they just need to hire a competent Chief Risk Officer (CRO). Dragonfly cautions that while appointing one is essential, it is unfortunately insufficient. One reason is the nature of the job; the other reason is signaling. The CEO, rather than the CRO, should decide what the "right" level and mix of risks should be. The decision is an integral component to the CEO's well-known roles in target-setting, strategy-making, resource allocation and managing his direct reports.

It may seem like a subtlety or semantics, but Dragonfly believes that the CEO must take a clear leadership role in risk management. The CRO should serve as the specialist who supports the CEO. The CRO provides dedicated focus and deep, specialized expertise. The function of the CRO is analogous to that of the CFO – although the CFO is the expert who runs the finance function, it is still the CEO who has to make the P&L and capital structure decisions.

When the CEO shows clear leadership in risk management, he is signaling to the entire organization that managing risk is also everyone's job, not just the CRO's. He is also asserting that risk management is not just about satisfying corporate governance or compliance needs. This is why Dragonfly believes that having **the CEO take a clear leadership role, is the single most important imperative for effective risk management**.

2. Expect Resistance, but Don't Wait for Buy-In

Many CEOs look for, or work hard to get buy-in on the need for risk management before they begin to develop and implement the capability. Few succeed. Many continue to look for and wait for the buy-in.

To get buy-in, many CEOs use some version of Control Self-Assessment (CSA) that involves conducting structured workshops where all department heads are required to identify and assess the risks within their own functions. The rationale is that, since the risk owners themselves perform the risk assessment, you would get their buy-in to the results.

Unfortunately, it never quite works that way. CSA approaches are tedious and few find the results useful. Hence in practice, you do not get buy-in for the process itself, even if there should logically be buy-in to the inputs. Many risk owners see it as an onerous compliance requirement imposed on them.

You Will Face Resistance

From our extensive experience, we can predict – confidently – that any development and implementation of risk management will face resistance. The only questions are, in what form, and to what degree. It may not be antagonistic, e.g., passive resistance, stalling, limiting attention or participation. Or it could be aggressive resistance – discrediting the methodology or results, withholding information, resisting changes or even outright hostility.

Implementing risk management is effecting change. It inevitably reduces autonomy. It will be intrusive. Hence, you *will* face resistance. You will not get buy-in. Even if a business line head feels that it is the right thing to do as a corporate citizen, he would resist in the interests of his own area.

Don't Wait for Godot, Start Anyway

Because of the inevitability of resistance, Dragonfly cautions against looking for buy-in before you start developing risk management. We recommend starting even though doing so appears counterintuitive. We advise our clients to go ahead and begin implementation, while at the same time expecting resistance and dealing with that accordingly. We are confident that buy-in can be secured in due course, but only once demonstrable results appear. Hence, the CEO is the one who needs to initiate the risk management development.

3. Minimize Reliance on Committees

Many CEOs form committees on the premise that this increases awareness and ownership of risks. On the surface, this looks promising because risk is taken by different functions within the organization, and decisions to mitigate or manage risks often involve tradeoffs that may favor one function or activity over another. It also often requires coordination across several functions.

While Dragonfly supports the use of committees to build organization-wide risk awareness, and for training in the common language and methodologies of risk management, the effectiveness of committees is limited.

For the identification, reporting, evaluation and management of risk, we do not recommend the use of committees. Instead of relying on committees, Dragonfly recommends using a combination of risk owners, risk specialists and the CEO:

- Front-line risk management is the responsibility of the direct risk owners — business lines, support functions. They structure and price the product. They manage the risks taken and operate their respective functions.

- The CRO and a team of risk specialists manage the policies required and the process of identifying, quantifying, reporting and evaluating all the risks enterprise-wide. The team provides comprehensive and timely data and analytics to support the CEO and his direct reports in risk decision-making.

- The CEO: As discussed earlier in the chapter, risk appetite and related risk management decisions are part of the CEO's job in setting targets, developing strategy and managing performance. Some CEOs prefer one-on-one sessions. Others may favor group meetings with multiple department heads. Whichever form is used, Dragonfly recommends that the CEOs, together with the risk owners, make the risk decisions — it should *not* be made by committees.

The right way to use a committee is for coordination, not for actual management of risks.

Enterprise-wide risk is the responsibility of the CEO supported by the CRO. Risks taken by business lines or functional heads are the responsibility of their respective areas. Therefore, risk cannot be "owned" by any committee.

66 Reading the Financial Times and the Wall Street Journal, you will notice that, again and again, there have been cases of failures in risk management -- not just at financial institutions, but also at companies in different sectors, government agencies and non-profit institutions. 99

4. Use Both Independence *and* Partnership

When asked, most CEOs and company directors would point out that the CRO should be clearly independent of the risk takers. We agree that this is a necessary condition to ensure the integrity of the risk data and prevent conflicts of interest. However, independence by itself is insufficient for effective risk management. Worse, it could even be dangerous.

In the course of our practice, we have encountered CROs who, in their quest to be independent, are so zealous that they act like risk "police". This creates animosity in the already inherently tense relationship between the CRO and the risk takers, who naturally do not like the reduced autonomy. The danger of a "cat and mouse" game or a "catch me if you can" mindset weakens risk management structurally, and often also insidiously.

Dragonfly recommends that the CRO act with *both* independence *and* with a partnership mindset. Being independent is well understood, and is necessary as stated earlier. But to be effective, we believe that the CRO has to find ways to be helpful to the risk takers – such as providing timely risk analytics and helping the business lines get approvals faster. This is the partnership mindset.

It may appear contradictory at first, but independence and a partnership mindset can co-exist. The CRO should be independent of the risk takers in the validation of data, in risk modeling and in risk analysis. But he or she can work in partnership with the risk takers to understand the needs and challenges they face in structuring products, pricing for the risks taken, and managing the risks involved in a cost-effective way. CROs can show empathy and be helpful, without compromising their independence and rigor.

In rare cases, some of the the risk takers may obfuscate, omit or hide risks outright, at least for some period of time. An independent CRO provides assurance to the firm that there is integrity in the risk data. But there is still the greater challenge of making sure that all risks are understood, and that no risk is omitted.

We advise clients to look for someone who is strong but without a big ego, who is confident but a good listener. The candidate must have the drive for excellence and rigor but not have a need to be liked or accepted. A CRO who is independent but collaborative, and analytically sharp but who does not act like a "risk buster", can help a CEO make risk management effective in practice.

> 66 All CEOs know that risks are
> taken by business lines, as well as by
> support functions throughout the firm.
> Unfortunately, not all CEOs appreciate
> that they 'inherit' -- and hence own
> -- all the risks taken by everyone,
> everywhere in the organization. 99

5. Data, Dialogue, Decisions

A critical principle of The Dragonfly Approach for making risk management effective is "Data, Dialogue and Decisions".

Data means having *all* risks identified and quantified. Dialogue means actually *using* risk data in discussions about strategic and operational decisions. Decisions means *making the judgment calls* about risk-return tradeoffs and risk appetite.

"Data, Dialogue, Decisions" has proven to be a powerful principle. We have used this for clients who are only beginning to develop risk management capabilities. We have also used this as a framework to diagnose and fix weakness in firms with well-established risk management processes.

For firms just starting to develop risk management, our approach is to get the risk data compiled first. This answers the question, "what bets are we taking?" It assembles the facts. It begins to build a common language for the organization — to identify and communicate about what risks are taken to get what business done.

With the risk data, we have something tangible to demonstrate the need for and benefits of a quantitative risk management process. This step can (and should) be completed without waiting for buy-in from the business lines. It speeds up the development of risk capabilities for the firm.

At the dialogue phase, we focus on making sure the risk data can be linked to the levers pulled by the business and support functions. This makes the discussions constructive and specific. We can ask key questions such as:

- What bets are we taking? For what purpose?
- How can we manage the bets adequately?
- Can we afford to take the bets?
- Can we handle the potential downside and volatility?

Data should be followed by dialogue, and by risk decisions – this is what makes risk management effective.

6. It is *Both* Science *and* Art

The CEO must understand that effective risk management is *both* science *and* art. There is a lot of science in risk management – the data, the math and statistics, the analytics. We need the science and the rigor, but CEOs should not expect the science to be prescriptive. The science cannot tell us what to choose, because risk, by definition, means we do not have certainty about what the "right" inputs are. That means we will not know what the "correct" decisions are.

For example, in evaluating strategic risk, we cannot know what our competitors will actually do. Hence we cannot know which strategic choice would be the "right" one.

At best, the science provides comprehensive and robust data and analytics — but using the risk data effectively is an art. It requires asking "what if's", selecting among tradeoffs, and deciding under uncertainty.

Once a CEO understands it is both science and art, he will not look for the "right answer". Instead he will systematically ask the "right questions". After that, he will make judgment calls, knowing that he will ultimately still be taking bets, but supported with the best science and data available.

7. Develop an Appropriate Risk Culture

The final imperative for effective risk management is that the CEO must develop a risk culture that fits the organization, the business and its strategy.

As CEO, you know what the prevailing organizational culture is. Who are the stars? What actions and achievements get the most favorable attention? How does information flow? What is considered risky? How do people feel about risk?

You also need to understand what type of risk-taking approach best fits the business environment you are in, and the strategies your firm and business lines are taking. Does your firm focus only on its core business? Is it opportunistic and does it make decisions rapidly? Do you have much complexity in your offerings? Is innovation a key strategic approach? These and related questions help determine the type of risk culture that is necessary for your organization to implement its strategies and manage the risks taken effectively.

For example, to succeed with an opportunistic strategy, you need an organization that uses a common risk language and is supported by comprehensive risk data. The firm also needs to be comfortable with debating risks and returns, and making decisions quickly, despite the uncertainty. As CEO, you need to pick the risk appetite and then act quickly.

Risk must be part of any firm's common language. Recognizing that we take bets in what we do and that we need to manage those bets actively must become part of *any* organizational culture.

Exhibit 9.2: Making Risk Management Effective

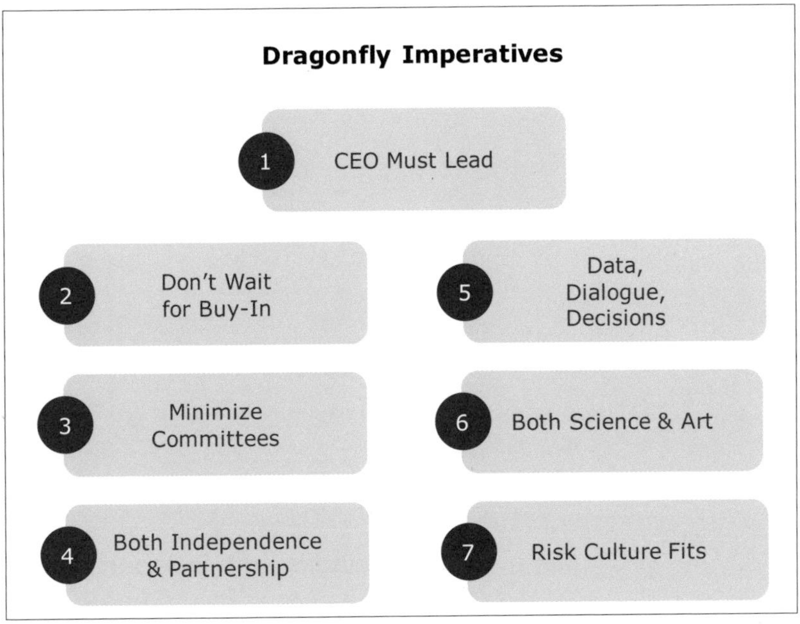

Dragonfly Imperatives

1. CEO Must Lead
2. Don't Wait for Buy-In
3. Minimize Committees
4. Both Independence & Partnership
5. Data, Dialogue, Decisions
6. Both Science & Art
7. Risk Culture Fits

Risk Insights from Chapter 9

Making Risk Management Effective in Practice

Most CEOs are aware of the need for risk management. In practice, however, the effectiveness of risk management functions at many organizations has been uneven.

Dragonfly believes there are 7 imperatives CEOs must adopt to ensure that risk management is effective:

1. The CEO must show clear leadership in risk management – that he ultimately owns all the risks and that managing risk is *his* job, supported by the CRO. This is in addition to the risk management practiced by the direct risk takers.

2. The CEO must not wait for buy-in. Instead he should commission the development of risk management right away, while expecting resistance from the organization. Buy-in will follow once results appear.

3. The CEO should minimize reliance on risk committees. Instead, the direct risk takers should perform frontline risk management; the CEO should manage risks at the enterprise level; and the CRO should focus on policies, methodology, risk analytics and reporting.

4. The CEO must pick a CRO who is *both* independent *and* can operate with a partnership mindset, i.e. helping the business lines structure and price risks better.

5. Data, Dialogue, Decisions: The CEO must ensure that comprehensive, timely risk data is produced, used in management dialogue, and that risk decisions are explicitly made.

6. The CEO must understand that effective risk management is *both* science *and* art – asking the "right" questions before making the judgment calls.

7. The CEO must develop a risk culture that fits the organization, the business and its strategy.

CONCLUSION

CONCLUSION:
THE NEXT FRONTIER —
INTEGRATING RISK, STRATEGY, FINANCE

We wrote this book to answer the fundamental questions CEOs ask about risk, such as:

- What must CEOs know about risk?
- What's the CEO's role in risk management?
- Can all risks be quantified?
- How to make the risk appetite decision?
- How to make sure risk management is effective in practice?

With the preceding 9 chapters, we have laid out The Dragonfly Approach to risk management. To recap, we believe that CEOs must know the following imperatives and insights about risk:

- Define risk appropriately - risk is the chance of not attaining your goals
- You are always taking bets
- You need to know your bets
- All risks must be quantified
- The shape and size of risk are driven by the exposure, sensitivity and size of shock
- All risks can be quantified

- Risk management should go beyond ensuring survival – it should minimize surprises, build resilience and enable the CEO to play offense
- You must use a common language for risk in your organization
- You must have a quantitative and explicit risk appetite decision process
- Be aware that some common risk methodologies are flawed, e.g. risk scores
- You must ensure that risk management in your firm is effective in practice
- The key deliverables for risk management are data, dialogue and decision making

The practice of risk management has come a long way since we started 25+ years ago. Today, almost all organizations have dedicated risk functions. Also, all firms have systematic strategic planning processes. And, all firms have comprehensive financial management capabilities.

In most organizations, however, risk is not integrated with strategy and finance. Risk often remains a standalone process, even at firms where risk management is well-resourced and sophisticated.

For example, all firms will conduct an annual strategic planning process, prepare budgets and financial plans. At well-run organizations, the thinking, analysis and implications of strategy and finance are linked and integrated, to a large extent. Substantial effort is made to iterate between deciding how the firm will compete, and what the financial performance could be, if that strategy is chosen. Although risk is considered, it rarely rises above a listing of various perils and mitigation measures. Risk is therefore not properly integrated with the disciplines of strategy or finance.

By integration, we mean:

- Incorporating risk identification, quantification and analysis directly into the strategy evaluation process. These should not be conducted only after the strategy has already been decided. The integrated approach is what what we call strategic planning under uncertainty.

- Incorporating risk drivers and the impact on the potential volatility of financial outcomes, directly in the financial planning and budgeting processes.

Strategy choices will be assessed, taking the relevant risk drivers into account. The potential impact of the risk drivers on the distribution of possible financial outcomes will be quantified and analyzed. Both strategy and finance decisions are assessed along side risk, which has been properly quantified. This is how strategy, risk and finance disciplines should be integrated.

Dragonfly believes that it is imperative for CEOs to integrate risk management with their firms' more longstanding strategy and finance practices. This is the next frontier for making risk management effective in helping CEOs lead and create value amid the heightened uncertainty and shocks that today's organizations face.

Exhibit 10.1
The Next Frontier: Integrating Risk, Strategy, Finance

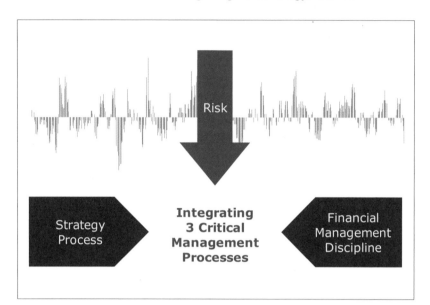

We hope that this book has answered most of your questions on what a CEO must know about risk. We appreciate your comments, ideas and further questions. We look forward to establishing a dialogue with you as we continue to push the frontiers in risk know-how and applications, to help CEOs keep their firms competitive and resilient under conditions of persistent volatility.

EXECUTIVE SUMMARY

1. Firstly, Define Risk Appropriately

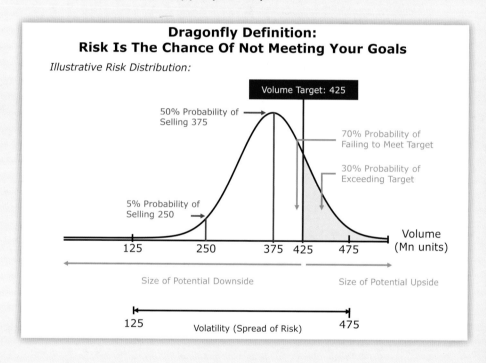

2. You Are Always Taking Bets

3. You Need to Know Your Bets

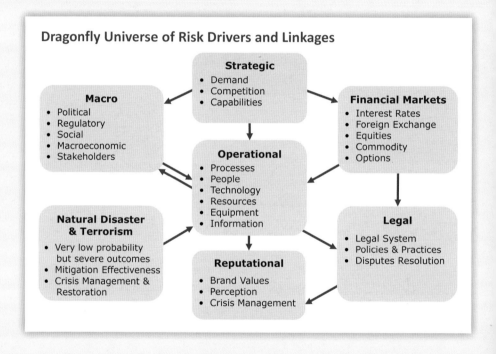

Dragonfly Universe of Risk Drivers and Linkages

Strategic
- Demand
- Competition
- Capabilities

Macro
- Political
- Regulatory
- Social
- Macroeconomic
- Stakeholders

Financial Markets
- Interest Rates
- Foreign Exchange
- Equities
- Commodity
- Options

Operational
- Processes
- People
- Technology
- Resources
- Equipment
- Information

Natural Disaster & Terrorism
- Very low probability but severe outcomes
- Mitigation Effectiveness
- Crisis Management & Restoration

Legal
- Legal System
- Policies & Practices
- Disputes Resolution

Reputational
- Brand Values
- Perception
- Crisis Management

4. Understand How Risks Are Created

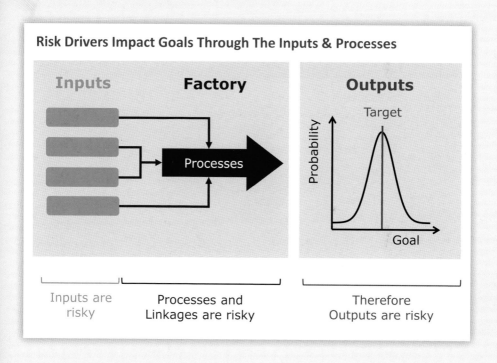

Risk Drivers Impact Goals Through The Inputs & Processes

| Inputs | Factory | Outputs |

Inputs are risky

Processes and Linkages are risky

Therefore Outputs are risky

5. All Risks *Must* Be Quantified

6. The Shape and Size of Risk Are Driven by 3 Factors

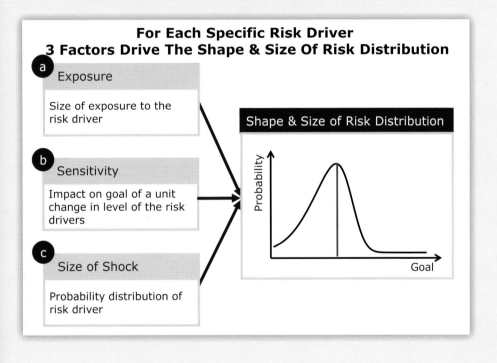

7. All Risks *Can* Be Quantified

Common Misconception That Some Risks Are Unquantifiable But Dragonfly Shows That All Risks *Can* Be Quantified

Examples of "Unquantifiable Risks"

- Reputational Risk
- Political Risk
- Operational Risk
- Non – Financial Risk

Underlying Problems

- Some risk types are "hard to quantify"
- One or more quantifiable steps not done
- Goals stated qualitatively
- Non-financial goals assumed to be qualitative

Dragonfly Approach

1. Apply The Dragonfly Risk Quantification Framework
2. Complete the quantification steps
3. Specify goals; restate quantitatively if necessary

8. Dragonfly Approach to Quantifying Strategic Risk

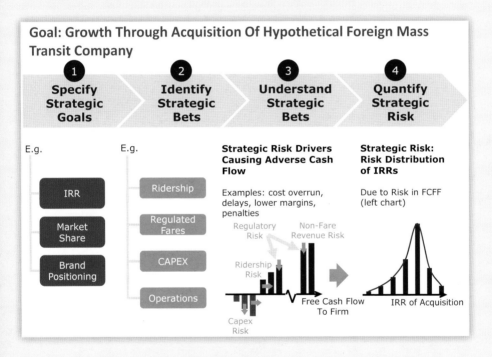

9. Decide What You Want Risk Management to Do

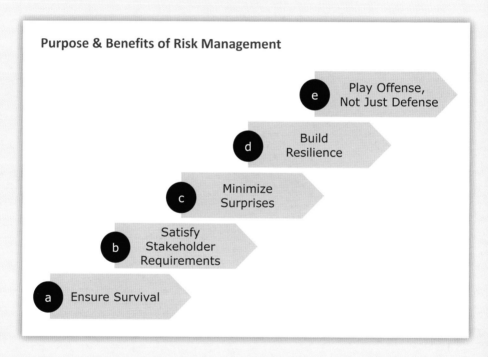

10. Clarify What Risk Management Is Not

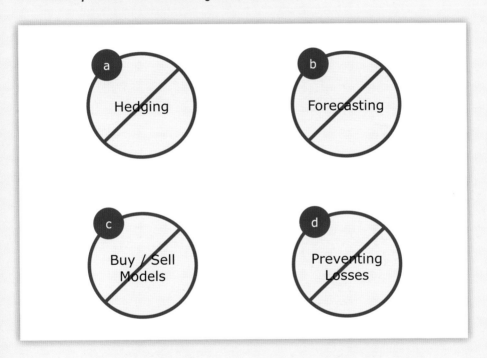

11. Use a Common Language for Risk Management in Your Organization

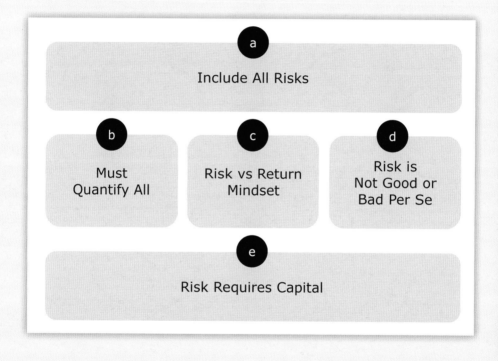

a
Include All Risks

b
Must Quantify All

c
Risk vs Return Mindset

d
Risk is Not Good or Bad Per Se

e
Risk Requires Capital

12. Show How You Make Risk Appetite Decisions

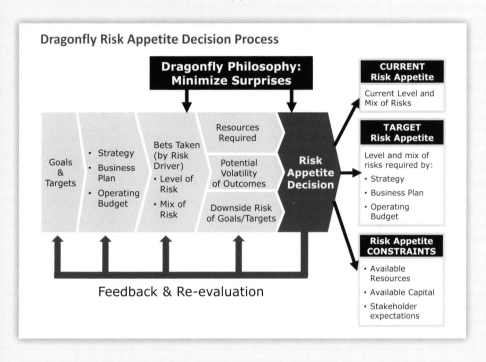

Dragonfly Risk Appetite Decision Process

13. Be Aware That Some Common Risk Practices Are Flawed

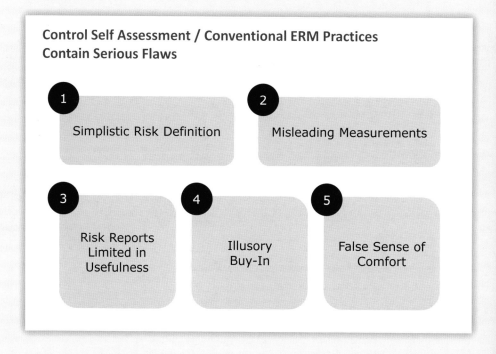

Control Self Assessment / Conventional ERM Practices Contain Serious Flaws

1. Simplistic Risk Definition

2. Misleading Measurements

3. Risk Reports Limited in Usefulness

4. Illusory Buy-In

5. False Sense of Comfort

14. The Commonly Used Risk Metric—Risk Score—Is Simplistic

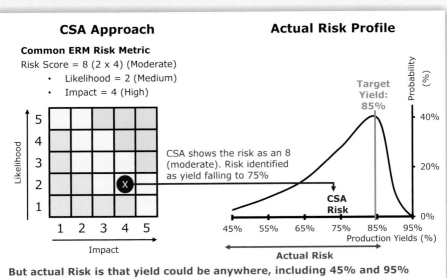

CSA Approach

Actual Risk Profile

Common ERM Risk Metric

Risk Score = 8 (2 x 4) (Moderate)
- Likelihood = 2 (Medium)
- Impact = 4 (High)

CSA shows the risk as an 8 (moderate). Risk identified as yield falling to 75%

Likelihood

Impact

Target Yield: 85%

Probability (%)

40%

20%

0%

CSA Risk

45%   55%   65%   75%   85%   95%

Production Yields (%)

Actual Risk

But actual Risk is that yield could be anywhere, including 45% and 95%
- Yield risk is a range of 45% to 85%, with upside of 95%
- Each yield has a different probability of occurrence
- Therefore a distribution is needed to fully profile the risk

15. Ultimately, You Must Ensure Your Risk Management Is Effective in Practice

Making Risk Management Effective: Dragonfly Imperatives For CEOs

1. CEO Must Lead
2. Don't Wait for Buy-In
3. Minimize Committees
4. Both Independence & Partnership
5. Data, Dialogue, Decisions
6. Both Science & Art
7. Risk Culture Fits

16. To Help CEOs Manage Uncertainty, the Dragonfly Risk Philosophy Provides Data, Dialogue & Decisions

17. CEOs Should Integrate Risk With Strategy & Finance

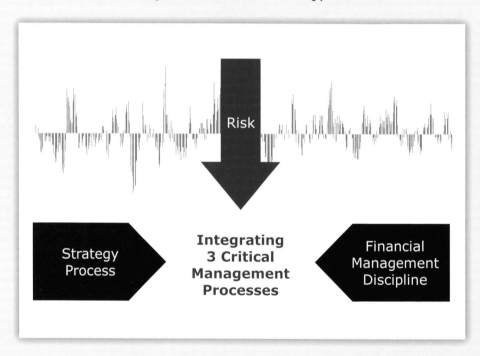

ACKNOWLEDGEMENTS

ACKNOWLEDGEMENTS

Writing this book has been a formidable challenge. Perhaps this is not surprising to many authors but it is astonishing to us, as going in we thought it would be hard, but "comfortably hard", to use a marathon running parlance. We already had more than enough content from 25+ years of both practitioner and advisory work in risk management. We have plenty of similar material we use for client assignments, for a university course we developed and taught, and for CEO seminars. We guessed that it would be more of a challenge to carve out enough time in our hectic client schedule and weekly international travel to select, structure and assemble the content into book form.

In writing this section and the last few pages of the book, we feel a strong mix of relief, accomplishment and gratitude. The first two are obvious. The latter, gratitude, we would like to elaborate on. Many people have helped us get the book started...and completed.

Khaimeng Wen, a CEO in the CapitaLand Group and one of our earliest clients was the first one to urge us to put The Dragonfly Approach to risk into book form. For years he would challenge, cajole and pressure us. Every holiday season he'd asked if we brought him "the present" – an advance copy of the Dragonfly book on risk.

We'd like to thank Danon The and Eharn Ng, two of Dragonfly's earliest associates who helped with much of the early research and book outline. They kept their enthusiasm and support for the book project long after they'd moved from Dragonfly to other fields.

We are grateful to Dr David Tan, Vice Dean and Professor at National University of Sinagpore Law School for providing intellectual guidance, editing and writing discipline right through to completion of the first draft. As a prolific published author himself David gave us powerful and authoritative tips on staying consistent in the writing process especially as we were constantly struggling to squeeze writing time from a packed schedule of client advisory engagements and business travel. Two of his many helpful admonishments: "Write something everyday, even if it's just one sentence"; "Don't try to write the final text. But write something. You cannot rewrite until you have first written the first version"

We want to thank Professor Soulaymane Kachani, Senior Vice Dean at Columbia University School of Engineering and Applied Sciences for thoroughly reading through the first draft and giving us thoughtful and critical comments. We have benefited from his questions and advice on content, structure and style.

Waihan Lock, currently CEO of a real estate development group read the first draft and gave us valuable comments from the perspective of a CEO and what a CEO wants to know and needs to know about risk.

We want to thank Swanfoo Boon, CEO of a fund and asset manager, and former CEO of ST Engineering Ltd for reviewing the draft of the book. We appreciate the insightful comments and questions from your perspective as a CEO and independent director in several sectors.

We'd like to thank Tsunyan Hsieh, a retired senior partner of McKinsey & Co for being an inspiration as a co-author of a leadership book, "Hearts, Smarts, Guts and Luck". He also generously shared advice on book writing, publishing and book marketing.

When we decided to write this book we aimed to put together the best answers to the most important questions CEOs have on risk. We also wanted it to be a good looking book — aesthetically pleasing from cover to layout, from fonts to exhibits. But we didn't realize how much imagination, skill and effort that would take. Lovelynne Chong, founder and CEO of Fyreflyz offered to help us make that happen from scratch. Together with Fenghui Zhuo, Fyreflyz created the first book cover design and full layout of the book. It gave us the first complete physical copies of the book.

Sweelin Lim, a longtime McKinsey & Co consultant helped us extensively in the editing and rewriting phase. Sweelin who wrote and published a book on nutrition and wellness, "10 Easy Habits of Eating Well Being Well" in less than a year, shared first hand and proven tactics for driving through the intense phase of finalizing the book.

We are grateful to Liengseng's daughters Nicole and Natalie — both helped with refining the chapter titles for clarity, punchiness and flow. Nicole reworked every exhibit from the first draft, challenging the captions, the graphics, the colours and the overall effectiveness as a visual aid. Natalie worked extensively on the book layout and the final cover design.

We'd like to thank Vinay Rai (introduced by Sweelin) for his advice on book editing, publishing and printing

Simon Siah found and arranged for us to meet top printing houses and guided us through the finer points of paper quality, color, weight and book binding.

We thank our editor Colin Goh for tirelessly and expertly editing the book. He tolerated the difficulties of working with an esoteric and fairly new field that is risk management. Colin deftly handled authors who resist making changes to the use of jargon arguing that "this field is different".

We thank Mike Ng of Mediasquare for doing the final book design and layout and taking it to the printing stage. Mike is not only incredibly competent, he is also personable and unflappable even with multiple changes and impossible deadlines.

We also want to thank different generations of Dragonfly associates who helped with aspects of the book.

There is a large number of people we need to thank – too many to name individually – for their contribution to the content of the book. We shall mention them in 4 groups: clients; CEOs/potential clients; risk managers; Bankers Trust colleagues.

Our clients at Dragonfly, Capco, Capital Markets Risk Advisors and Bankers Trust gave us the opportunities to develop risk management solutions for different industries and refine our methodologies and know how to what has become The Dragonfly Approach.

We would like to thank the numerous CEOs, CFOs and company directors we have had the opportunity to discuss risk management with, and in some cases do work for. Your objectives and issues, your questions on what you need to know about risk inspired the title and structure of this book.

We owe many risk management specialists we have met or worked with, a special thank you. Thirty years ago, risk management did not exist as an area of specialist know how or discipline (outside of the insurance sector). This growing group of risk specialists developed, tested and applied the discipline, starting with financial institutions before steadily expanding into other sectors. This book draws from this pool of expertise and experience.

Our own experience originated with the pioneering efforts at Bankers Trust. There are too many people to thank but we must specifically mention a few, starting with Charlie S Sanford, Jr. While transforming a commercial bank into a global investment bank with strong trading and capital markets capabilities, he commissioned the development of a pioneering enterprise risk management methodology that is quantitative, covers all risks and is linked to earnings and capital. Charlie hired Liengseng to the bank where he worked with Daniel Mudge, head of Global Risk Management. Tim Yates who was CFO, Dan Borge who was head of Corporate Strategy, Clinton Lively, a fellow managing director in Global

Risk and Gene Shanks, President of Bankers Trust were all colleagues we worked closely with in developing and applying risk management across the bank.

Before we close, we feel it might be interesting to some of our readers to mention where this book was created. Ninety percent of the book was written, rewritten and edited in cafes and airplane cabins, especially on the 10,000 mile trip between New York City and Singapore. Somehow it always seemed that we were more creative and productive at coffee shops and 30,000 feet in the air. Geographically, the book was created mostly in New York City, Silicon Valley, Tokyo and Singapore.

One hundred percent of the book was first written by hand, on physical paper. It seems archaic but it allowed us to indulge in Moleskine and other fine notebooks, blank writing cards and a collection of fountain pens. This aspect of writing the book was always so much fun.

ABOUT THE AUTHORS

ABOUT THE AUTHORS

 **JUDY LEE** is co-founder and partner at Dragonfly LLC, a New York based advisory firm founded in 2000 that provides strategy, risk management and investment evaluation to CEOs in all industry sectors worldwide.

Judy is a pioneer and leader in risk management starting as a key member of the team that developed the risk methodology at Bankers Trust in the late 1980s. She also worked on financial derivatives and capital markets products.

After Bankers Trust, Judy was a partner at two international risk advisory firms in New York – Capital Market Risk Advisors and Capco – before co-founding Dragonfly.

Judy was an adjunct professor at Singapore Management University where she taught Enterprise Risk Management for 10 years – a course she and Liengseng Wee developed.

Judy is a director on the Board of Temasek Lifesciences Accelerator. She also serves on the Board of Overseers of New York University Stern School. She has served on the board of directors at Solar Frontier, a subsidiary of Showa Shell Sekiyu KK that makes solar panels and develops solar power plants.

Judy has an Executive MBA from the Wharton School and a BS from New York University Stern School. She lives in New York City when she is not traveling to clients in US and Asia.

LIENGSENG WEE is CEO and co-founder of Dragonfly LLC. He was a partner and head of the strategy and risk management practice at Capco, an international financial services solutions firm. Prior to that he was a partner at Capital Markets Risk Advisors in New York City.

Liengseng was a managing director in Global Risk Management at Bankers Trust where he helped to develop and run the enterprise risk function. He also co-headed the bank's Risk Advisory group that provided risk analysis and solutions for the bank's clients.

Liengseng was a strategy consultant with Booz Allen, based in New York City. Prior to that he was a banker with Banque Paribas based in Singapore.

Liengseng was an adjunct professor at Singapore Management University where he taught Enterprise Risk Management for 10 years -- a course he and Judy developed.

Liengseng has an MBA with Distinction from the Wharton School and a BBA from the National University of Singapore.

He is based in New York City and "commutes" weekly to clients in US, Tokyo, Singapore and other cities in Asia.